THE TIMES OF INDIA

THE BEST OF
SPEAKING
TREE

VOLUME 3

THE TIMES OF INDIA

THE BEST OF
SPEAKING
TREE

VOLUME 3

THE BEST OF SPEAKING TREE - Volume 3

Copyright ©Bennett, Coleman & Co., Ltd., 2006

Published in 2006

Sixth reprint in 2013

by
Bennett, Coleman & Co., Ltd.
7, Bahadur Shah Zafar Marg
New Delhi-110002

Acknowledgements
We thank all those who have contributed to "The Speaking Tree" column in
The Times of India over the years.

Edit, Design, Marketed and Distributed by

Times Group Books
(A division of Bennett, Coleman and Company Limited)
Times Annexe, 9-10, Bahadur Shah Zafar Marg, New Delhi-110002

ISBN 978-93-80942-08-7

Printed by
International Print-o-Pac Ltd.

Price: ₹250

Preface

N the spiritual, the transcendent, have a place in something that of necessity has to be so topical and time bound a forum as a newspaper? We in *The Times of India* believe that the answer is an emphatic 'yes'. For, we believe that the legitimate realm of the spiritual is not in sequestered monasteries or in the lofty towers of philosophical thought alone. It is very much an integral part of our lives, of our thoughts and actions, and can motivate in us right personal, social and political impulses. We cannot avoid or escape these daily Kurukshetras of the mind and the soul. All we can hope to do, as Arjuna did with the help of Krishna, is to learn to realise that while we must act in the face of moral and ethical ambiguities we can try and do so without the material attachments alone determining our actions. This is where *The Speaking Tree* provides a grove of contemplative tranquillity, a sanctuary of the spirit where we can find strength to face anew the conflicts and the confrontations that are part of our human predicament. While occasionally eminent seers have contributed to *The Speaking Tree* column, most often, it is the so-called common citizen who is the author of these pieces — which is as it should be. For the world of the spirit is not out there or invested in some teacher or guru; it is our common heritage, ours to claim and ours to nurture. Welcome to its shade.

Indu Jain

New Delhi
April 2006

Content

Cosmic Trumpeting of Lord Ganapati

By K M Gupta

THE origin of the concept of Ganapati, the elephant-headed God, is related to the origin of the universe. What was the origin of the universe? The universe was not there in the beginning. Or, if it were there, what had become of it? One view is that it had shrunk to a bindu. Bindu means point. The universe had contracted to a point. That is just its way. Now it contracts; now it expands. It is a perpetual cycle stretched over billions of human years.

Expansion is creation and contraction is dissolution. In geometry, a point has position but no dimensions. The position of a thing is in relation to other things in space. Since bindu is the contraction of the whole universe, of the whole time-space-mind continuum, it can have no position. Since it has no dimensions, and since it is the contraction of time-space-mind, the mind just cannot grasp it. For the three-dimensional mind to grasp a thing, that thing, too, has to be 3-D. For the mind, a thing without dimensions doesn't exist at all.

That's why the bindu is beyond comprehension and equal to nothing. For the bindu to burst into being again, to stretch out its withdrawn dimensions and thus to expand again, it needs a bang-start. The spark for this bang-start comes in the form of desire. The bindu desired to expand again, to burst into being again, to be manifest and to multiply. Desire heated it up to a fireball bursting with desire. At the extreme height of heat and pressure, it just exploded. This explosion of bindu is called Bindu Visphota. The explosion stretched forth, well outside its withdrawn dimensions. It started to expand. It ceased to be nothing. It bounced back into being.

The present 3-D space is the volume expansion of bindu. This volume expansion is called Saguna (dimensioned) Brahmn. This Saguna Brahmn is the 3D-isation of Nirguna (dimensionless) Brahmn, that is, the original bindu. Saguna Brahmn and Moola

8

Prakriti (the original nature) are one and the same. Shankara has acknowledged their being synonymous. All that occupies the 3-D space is its own local temporary warps. Warping or curvature of space-time is called vivarta.

By warping itself, Nature creates all. Space is prakriti; it is occupied by its own vikriti (deformity). This, in essence, is the cosmogony and cosmology of Vedanta. The sound of the initial explosion, the bang-start of bindu, was likened to the trumpeting of an elephant. Bindu trumpeted like a cosmic elephant in the beginning, and the universe is the 3-D expansion of the sound energy of that initial cosmic trumpeting.

In Sanskrit, the word for the trumpeting of an elephant is brimhita or brihatika. The word Brahmn was originally derived from this brimhita. Bindu, the spacestuff, is Brahmn, and Brahmn is a cosmic elephant making a cosmic trumpeting to inaugurate Creation. Since this cosmic elephant is the cause and Lord of all ganas — groups, bonds, assemblages — in the universe, it was called Ganapati. That is the origin of the concept of Ganapati or Ganesha.

We are familiar with Ganapati Mandala, a diagram consisting of two transverse equilateral triangles with a point in the middle. The point in the middle is bindu, the trumpeting elephant. The two transverse triangles with their six vertices represent the volume expansion of bindu — the emergence of the 3-D space, of moola prakriti, of creation. What expands bindu into volume is its big brimhita bang, represented by the space enclosed by the transverse triangles and surrounding bindu.

The Whys and Hows of Life on Earth

By Sadhguru Jaggi Vasudev

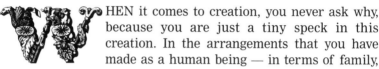 HEN it comes to creation, you never ask why, because you are just a tiny speck in this creation. In the arrangements that you have made as a human being — in terms of family, your social structures, your financial securities, education, qualifications and positions that you have taken in the society — I know you slowly started assuming that, in many ways, you are the centre of the universe. But that is not the truth.

You might have created so many comforts, so much security, but still the inherent struggle of it, the inherent pain of it, the day-to-day tensions, remain. You fill yourself with enthusiasm; you find new reasons for yourself to do this and that.

But somewhere inside there is something which constantly struggles in every human being unless he attains a certain inner grace. Till then, the struggle continues. Some people have become aware of it; most people haven't. They just keep themselves busy, never to face the inner struggle.

The reason why people are keeping themselves so busy, so entangled with life is not because they have fallen in love with life. It is just to avoid the inner struggle. Many of them, if they don't get married and produce children, if they don't start businesses and don't get into all the mess that they are getting into on a day-to-day basis, they would be simply lost within themselves.

Just to keep a certain semblance of sanity, they keep all this activity going. If they just sit quietly for two days in one place, they will become aware of the inner struggle that is there in every being trapped in this limited body. It is always there. Some become aware.

Once they become aware, they start looking. That is when we say somebody is on the spiritual path, because he has become aware of the inner struggle. No matter what you do, something is struggling within all the time. But others are still too busy.

So the question comes up because there is an inner struggle. Maybe you are not 100 per cent aware of the struggle, but here and there it touches you. So now, the more intelligent question for you would be: How do I get beyond this struggling state? If you ask how, I have a way. If you ask why, then I have to tell you a story. One day, Shiva had nothing to do and he was playing marbles all by himself. And one marble fell this way and it became planet Earth.

Another one shot up and it became the Sun; I can go on like this. Now you won't believe this ridiculous story. But if I make the story more elaborate, and if the story is not told today, but was said 1,000 years ago, you would believe it. You have a problem about this, isn't it? You don't believe anything that happens today, but you will believe it after 1,000 years. It doesn't matter what it is.

So, if it was said 1,000 years ago... you would believe the story. But stories don't liberate you. Stories just equip you to speak with some sense of authority at the next dinner party you are invited to. But it won't liberate you in any way. So when it comes to existence, don't waste your life asking the question, "Why?"

Because if you sit here for the rest of your life and go on thinking why, or consult every other man on this planet, all you will get is more and more fairy tales; you will not get a solution.

Different cultures will tell different stories; different religions will tell different stories; every individual can create his own story. Stories will not liberate you. But if you ask "How", then we open up the Path, we give you the method. Don't ask "Why?"

The Cosmic Force and Shiv-Shakti

By Yogiji

EFORE creation took place there was nothing but a pervading consciousness that had no name. Creation was the result of manifestation of this pervading consciousness. The first form in which the consciousness manifested was Adi Shakti, Gayatri or power. From her emerged everything else.

Once the universe was created there was a need for super forces or energies to look after the governance of the world. To perform this role Adi Shakti manifested herself into the trinity: Brahma, Vishnu and Shiva. Brahma is the energy responsible for creation of the physical world. Brahma along with his consort Saraswati gave birth to everything that exists in entire creation — every word, sound, and each and every imaginable, unimaginable, perceivable or imperceptible object and being.

Vishnu along with Lakshmi became the energy responsible for the maintenance of the world. They govern the cycle of karma. Maya is his tool. It keeps all the souls engaged in a cycle of karma. But certain souls want to go beyond this cycle of karma. They seek the blessings of Ardhanareeshwar, the energy responsible for transformation. Those who have realised the futility of the physical and material world go back to their source with the blessings of Shiva.

Ardhanareeshwar is the form representing Shiva and Shakti as One. These energy forces reside in each one of us, providing us with the power to overcome all karmas. With the practice of yoga or union with the Divine, one can realise and develop one's power to raise consciousness beyond the veil of maya and return to godhead, the source we came from.

After the emergence of the trinity, the physical world was given form. Consciousness manifested itself into two more forms to create the physical prana as jad, the five elements — air, water, ether, earth and fire — and prana as chetan or awakened consciousness. Prana is both jad and chetan, in varying combinations. Existing at varying frequencies it gives shape to each and every physical thing of the universe; prana is the Force in the universe.

The Force has a unique frequency. In human form prana combines itself with the elements to form energy centres called chakras. Each main chakra represents a human characteristic such as emotion, power and physical strength. Evolution in human form is a process of rising above each chakra and this is possible only when one has complete control over all human functions or qualities. Only then a person is entitled to transformation to a higher level of consciousness.

In this entire process the force that rises up and travels through each chakra to help a human being go through evolution is the kundalini force. Kundalini is pure power or Shakti, which resides in each one of us in a dormant form in the lowest chakra. For evolution and transformation this force needs to be awakened to achieve Yoga, the union with Divine.

Shakti can be awakened and brought up through the chakras only with the help of Shiva, who resides in the highest human chakra. Shiva has to come down himself to awaken Shakti and unite with her at every level to enable transformation. Their union generates the power that enables evolution to take place at each chakra — that is, the yogi overcomes desires controlled by that chakra. Since Kundalini is pure power, if awakened in an uncontrolled manner, it can destroy the human body beyond repair. A guru's guidance is therefore essential.

Creative Math of the Origins of Universe

By T S Rajagopalan

OR the creation of anything, three causes are required to be fulfilled: material cause, instrumental cause and supporting cause. In Creation, Brahmn is all of these three causes. He evolves Himself into Mulaprakriti or primordial matter. At the time of pralaya, Prakriti is in a subtle, undifferentiated state, avibhakta. When matter evolves from its dormant initial state, tattva mahat or reality comes out. From mahat, we get the tattva ahankara. Both mahat and ahankara are of three kinds: sattvika, rajasa and tamasa, based on qualities.

From sattvika ahankara we get all the senses or indriyas of knowledge and karma. So we have five jnana indriyas, five karma indriyas and the mind, bringing the total to 11.

Next, from tamasa ahankara the sabda tanmattra or the subtle element of sound is created, from which the gross element of ether is produced. From this is produced the subtle element of touch, sparsa, which, in turn, produces the gross element of air, vayu.

This produces the subtle element of sight, rupa, which produces the gross element of light, tejas. From this is created the subtle element of taste, rasa, and thereon, the gross element of water and then the subtle element of smell, gandha. Finally, from this is produced the gross element of earth, prithvi. So each of the subtle elements, tanmattra, is an intermediate stage of creation between two gross elements, bhutas.

The stages are: prakriti or matter, mahat, ahankara, sound, ether, touch, air, sight, light, taste, water, smell and earth. So in the process of creation we have 24 items, beginning with 1) empirical or fundamental matter, 2) mahat, 3) ahankara, 4-8) the five subtle elements, 9-13) the five gross elements, pancha bhutas, 14) the mind, 15-19) the senses of knowledge, and 20-24) the karma indriyas, bringing the total number of elements to 24. Number 25 is the jivatma and 26, the Brahmn.

Still further evolutionary progress is called panchi-karana or quintuplication, the five-fold division. Here, a bit of mathematics is involved. Each gross element is taken and divided into two halves. One half of this element is split up into four equal parts and added to the other remaining four gross elements. For example, take ether, one of the gross elements, and divide it into two halves. One half of it is further divided into equal portions, namely, 1/8th each and so 1/8th ether is added to each of the remaining gross elements — air, light, water and earth.

In the same way the remaining four gross elements are also divided into halves and each half is again divided into four portions and added to the other gross elements. This principle has been cited in a verse by Tamil saint Thirumazhisai Alwar.

There is another process called trivitkarana or trifold division. The same procedure is applied in regard to three gross elements, namely light, water and earth. The gross element of light will consist of 50 per cent light, 25 per cent water and 25 per cent earth. Vishnupurana describes saptikarana or seven-fold division where along with the five gross elements the two earlier tattvas mahat and ahankara are also added.

The principle of division is the same. There are two types of creation, samashti srishti, aggregate creation and vyashti srishti, individual creation — the creation of mahat out of prakriti, of ahankara and the 10 indriyas of knowledge and karma, of panchabhutas and subtle elements. All these are called aggregate creation.

This is how the world or the universe was created. The further creation of human beings, animals, trees and plants is called individual creation.

The World as the Vikings Saw It: Chaos to Cosmos

By Narayani Ganesh

ONG before the people of Scandinavia took to Christianity, pagan Nordic spirituality had its own view of Creation. Indigenous Nordic peoples' perception of the spiritual universe is sourced from poems and folklore that have survived through oral tradition since the time of the Vikings.

Snorri Sturluson, the 12th century Icelandic chieftain, devoted to literature and scholarship compiled poems and stories (The Edda) that reflect the spiritual beliefs of the Vikings, their gods and goddesses, detailing the creation of the world and the deeds of the gods.

A description of what prevailed before chaos and the creation of heaven, earth and seas talks about the great abyss, the Ginnungagap, without form and void.

Like the Rig Vedic hymn that describes the Beginning, the following Nordic verse resounds with philosophic profundity: "In the beginning/ not anything existed,/ there was no sand or sea/ nor cooling waves;/ earth was unknown/ and heaven above/ only Ginnungagap/ was — there was no grass".

On either side of the great abyss lay Muspellheim, the land of fire, and Niflheim, the land of ice. A spirit, Fimbultyr, moved upon the face of the abyss and the movement made the rivers of fire and ice collide. As they flowed into the abyss, the melting and melding gave birth to the sleeping giant, Ymir.

Ymir was the first living creature, ancestor of the evil race of giants. From his different body parts were created male and female beings who started the race of frost giants. So out of chaos were born evil giants, conjured from a cosmic soup of fire and ice, with a spirit breathing life into them.

The giant Ymir sustained himself by drinking the milk dripping from the teats of the cosmic cow, Audhumla, who was also a creation of melting ice. The cow, in turn, lived by licking the salty blocks of ice which, when melted, revealed a male figure, Buri. He married Bestla the giantess and fathered three sons, the Aesir gods, and the first of whom was Odin, the first Nordic God. The gods lived in Asgard, a Divine City.

The spirit, Fimbultyr, ordered that Ymir be slain so that chaos could be replaced by order. Odin and his brothers mortally wounded Ymir and from his body they made the universe. His flesh yielded the earth, his blood became the sea, rocks formed from his bones, his hair became trees, his skull the vaulted heavens and from his eyebrows formed Midgard, the eternal stronghold.

The gods made man and woman in their own image from two trees, breathing into them the breath of life. The living souls, Ask and Embla, inhabited a garden where their children grew up and survived for generations till the end of time. Cosmos was thus created.

The theme of Nordic spirituality is that the past is the mirror that reflects the future. The Tree that stands for light, life and order symbolises the quest for knowledge. The cosmic tree's branches spread out over the whole world and reach up to heaven. Its roots extend also to the abode of humans and to the deep abyss from whence chaos began and within its roots lay Mimir, the owner of the fountain of wisdom.

Inspired by Faith in the Sun and the Moon

By Sudhamahi Regunathan

OFTEN, we are tempted to dismiss tribal faiths as primitive and so of considerably less philosophical and spiritual content than organised faiths. At the same time, even those just faintly acquainted with tribals speak highly of their honesty and the absence of guile. If faith plays any role in developing the moral calibre of a society, surely, tribal faiths should be credited with more power and content.

One such faith, which seems well developed and has many oral texts that are beautiful, is the faith of the tribals of Arunachal Pradesh. Today the tribes have given it a name: Donyipoloism. Only the name is new. Their sacred texts called aabangs are as old as the hills and they have in them the magic that lends itself graciously to piety. It has also served them well in the difficult conditions on the eastern Himalayas where life is hard and cold.

This faith is professed by five major tribes in Arunachal Pradesh. These five major tribes, the Adis, the Apatanis, the Tagins, the Nishis and the Hill Miris constitute more than one-half of Arunachal Pradesh's population and are located in the central part of the state.

The five tribes are also grouped together as the Tani group for they all believe themselves to be descendants of Abo Tani, the first man. Tani mythology says that the beginning was nothingness. A vacuum with no attributes, existent and yet non-existent, the whole and yet nothing — a concept very similar to the Vedic one. From this nothingness, Keyum, came beings.

Loosely translated, this is described in the sacred text, aabang, as: "Oh! How to begin and create the story/ Keyum and Kero are pregnant with silence/ Oh! it is not known how to move the story further/ Keyum and Kero is all/ silence and vacuum/ Keyum is unknown,/Unknowable./Kero is invisible/ and unfathomable..."

It continues in this strain describing the Keyum-Kero of no attributes. "Absolute silence without echo or answer: in course of

18

time, the unknown and the unexplored void was filled with friction and vibrations and that which was neither seen nor unseen began to evolve into being."

The stages and manner of evolution of the universe from this vacuum are told differently by each tribe. But this beginning is rarely invoked in prayers. Generally all prayers reach the Supreme, the Ultimate reality through Donyipolo. Donyipolo was the energy that caused the vibrations in Keyum. And with the vibrations, many creations sprung up, the earth, the other planets, the stars and the sun and the moon.

The Adi-Minyong myth on the creation of Donyi and Polo, says that the eyes of a giant figure went up into the sky as the 'suns'. A similar concept is found in many of the Upanishads, of the sun and moon being the eyes of a great cosmic being. "One was Donyi and the other was Polo. The universe had swinging power and so as the eyes separated, they continued rotating and so revolve one after another." Donyi and Polo, individually mean the sun, Donyi, and the moon, Polo.

They are viewed as manifestations of the divine who watch over this world. Physically they are the link between the supreme and the mortal world. At the metaphysical level Donyi and Polo acquire another meaning when they come together as Donyipolo. The attributes of Donyipolo are different from the individual figures they represent. It forms a force that is self- motivating, creative, energising and all-powerful.

The combination of the male and female element emerges as the force that is most powerful. They cease to describe the physical manifestations of the celest ial objects. Together they represent a great energy and symbolise the source of truth, justice, morality and goodness. An energy that moves the world. An idea very similar to that of prakriti and purusha or yin and yang.

The belief in Donyipolo is manifest in the everyday life of the Tani group. Donyi is invoked for anything and everything and by everyone. The most common exclamation is, Donyi-e-kalangka: the sun shall see. This cry heralds the proceedings of all activity seeking to mete justice. Donyipolo is thus called upon as the highest judicial authority.

There are many versions of the following Adi saying which captures the essence of Donyi and Polo in Tani mythology: "The sun rays will not slip off the right path nor will the moon rays hide behind a cloud." The moral is to emulate them in righteousness and courage. Donyipolo are the twin aspects of everything in life.

The Purpose of Our Life is to 'Know'

By Swami Sunirmalananda

CREATION is an ocean of surprises. Just see the little planet in the universe — our world, the earth. Count the variety of living and non-living things here. From amoeba to elephant, the variety is simply astonishing.

But there are five vital questions about creation. The first one is, who created this universe? Religion says that there is a God, but the scientist has not fully accepted it. The second question is, why has this universe been created? No one can answer this question. The third one is, when was this universe created? Again, the answer is a big 'we don't know'. No doubt modern physicists are trying to calculate the date of creation, but they are vacillating. The fourth question is, out of what has this universe been created? No answer again, though both philosophers and scientists have broken down solid mass into the atom and say it is the fundamental unit of life. That, though, is not the final answer. Thus, the four vital questions have remained unanswered till now.

Precise answers like 'Milk is white' are yet to come. This brings us to the fifth and final question: 'What's our role in creation?' The first possible rational answer is, we do not have any role at all. Like all living beings, we are born, undergo metamorphosis, and die. But is that all? Are we mere waves in the ocean? Fortunately not. Why, because human beings alone ask questions. We alone can raise the above five vital questions about creation. So we are unique beings and have a unique role to play in creation.

What is that role? That unique role is to know. Humans alone can know. Sri Ramakrishna says: "God no doubt dwells in all, but He manifests Himself more through man than through other beings. Is man an insignificant thing? He can think of God, he can think of the Infinite, while other living beings cannot."

But what is the use of knowing? Knowledge brings liberation from existential suffering. How do we know? There are two methods: one of science, and other of religion. Science is the study of the external; religion is the study of the internal. The first is objective while the second, subjective. But is not science, the objective study of the universe, right since we wish to know the universe?

Scientists too thought they alone were right, but many are differing now. Consciousness and universe, they see, are interwoven. Since ages, science has accumulated much knowledge about the earth, solar system, stars, and galaxies. And they have propounded many theories.

However, yesterday's theory is today's junk. Why, because the more we study, the more it is confusing, and more is left unknown. Secondly, the instrument, the mind, can't find answers to all our questions through the five senses.

This leads us to the second path: religion. Religion alone has declared that the universe is only an objective manifestation of the subjective. Let us never think that the scenes we see on the big screen are real; there is the projector behind.

Religion is the study of man: an in-depth study. This study leads to supreme knowledge of everything. How? It was Swami Vivekananda who experienced the grandest truth that, "The microcosm and the macrocosm are built upon the same plan."

To know the human being is to know the universe. But to know the human being you don't need instruments. The fine instrument called mind will suffice. Using it, we have to dive deep into ourselves: we should meditate. Meditation leads us to the hitherto unseen universe within. The inner universe, say saints, is astounding. This universe will reveal all the knowledge we need. This, again, will free us. The knowledge of why, who, how, what, etc. will all become perfectly clear once we look within. Sri Ramakrishna declared: "A man attains everything when he discovers his true Self in himself. That also is the purpose of assuming a human body." Shankaracharya sang that human birth is the most precious gift of God. To expand it in vain pursuits is a colossal and stupendous waste. To utilise it is to know the greatest good. Therefore, let us all sit down quietly for sometime every day, close our eyes, and dive deep within. This alone, and nothing else, will bring us knowledge, lasting peace and supreme happiness.

We Create Our God, Only to Kill Him

By Jug Suraiya

HEN Voltaire remarked that if God did not exist we would have had to invent Him, the clever Frenchman almost got it right. Instead of 'if' he ought to have used 'as': As God did not exist, we had to invent Him. For the so-called Creator is nothing but our creation, like a conjurer's illusion. And like an amnesic conjurer who has forgotten his own sleight of hand, we take the illusion for reality.

This gives rise to a number of problems, metaphysical and moral. For instance, scholastics in mediaeval Europe would engage in endless debate about God's omnipotence and the paradoxes it led to. Could God build a wall so high that He could not jump over it? If He were omnipotent, He could build such an unjumpable wall. But by the same token of his omnipotence, He could jump over it.

What the debaters did not see was that both the Wall, and its Athletic Builder, were equally figments of their imagination. As was the debate. The moral problems of God's existence centre around the question: If a benevolent and all-powerful God exists, why does He allow bad things to happen to good people? The answer often provided is that it's all part of a Divine Plan which we can't see and therefore can't understand. Unfortunately, this makes God sound like an Orwellian Big Brother who works strictly on a need-to-know basis while manipulating our minds and actions.

A far more elegant 'solution' to the problem would be to see that the 'bad' things that happen are a result not of a malevolent, inscrutable fate but simply of our own attachment. From the perspective of perfect detachment both 'bad' things and 'good' things disappear.

Then there is the problem of prayer and the role of God as an interventionist in our affairs. If I say my prayers and observe the scriptures, surely God will make my wishes come true. But what if those wishes include my triumph over my neighbour, an equally devout and pious individual who wishes to triumph over me?

What'll God do? Ignore us both? In which case, why are we wasting our time? Or will he leave it all to chance to see which of us wins over the other? In which case, He becomes nothing but a lottery ticket in the sky. So what's the answer? Perhaps that our concepts of 'triumph' and 'defeat', not to mention 'rival', 'piety', 'prayer', and 'God' Himself, are limited and limiting constructs of our own mind.

We create God in our own image. Auden wrote: "O God, put away justice and truth for we cannot understand them and do not want them. Eternity would bore us dreadfully. Become our uncle. Look after baby, amuse grandfather, introduce Muriel to a handsome officer. Be interesting and weak like us, and we will love you as we love ourselves."

The ancient gods — of Indic or Greek mythology — were whimsical, lustful, mendacious. Just like their worshippers, just like us. Perfect soap opera material for pre-TV days. The Jehovah of the Old Testament was a vengeful, bloodthirsty scourge, reflecting militant tribalism. The New Testament, with its message of peace and goodwill, was the precursor of the MNC: God as a global franchiser, a spiritual counterpart of McDonald's.

When the West got tired of its God, it killed Him via Nietzsche. We have killed God, said the philosopher and unleashed existential angst among his contemporaries. Ramakrishna was much cooler about it. In meditation, when his beloved Mother appeared before him he took the sword of duality and cut Her in two, severing the bonds of his worship.

Had Voltaire been around, would he have said: If God did not exist, we would have had to destroy Him?

Universe is Brahmn in Disguise

By K M Gupta

EDANTA is about neither theism nor atheism. Or, to put it another way, it is atheism in theism and theism in atheism. We will see how. According to Vedanta, Brahmn is the ultimate character or structure of the universe. In fact, the universe is Brahmn in disguise.

When the universe is reduced to its starkest nakedness, it is Brahmn. Therefore 'I am Brahmn' (aham brahmasmi), 'you are Brahmn' (tatwam asi), 'all are Brahmn' (sarvam khalu idam brahma). Just what is this Brahmn? The Brihadaranyaka, Chandogya and Taittiriya Upanishads make it plain and clear that Brahmn is akasha — that is, space, Kham brahma, akasho vy nama brahma... When the Isha Upanishad says that it is the inside of all and the outside of all, it means space. Literally also, Brahmn is space. Brahmn is "the largest and the ever-enlargening", "that which contains all but is not contained by anything".

Brahmn or space was just a point in the beginning, before Creation. A point, as we learn in our geometry class, has no dimensions. As it is dimensionless, it is called nirguna or without attributes. Nirguna Brahmn is space without dimensions — that is, space contracted to a point.

Then this point — referred to as akshara, matra, bindu or shukra — exploded. The cause for the explosion is kama or libido. Kama is the primeval and eternal force. It is this primeval force that manifests itself as all the forces in the world. Kama is the creator. Kama is one with the point. The explosion of the point is the burst of kama.

The explosion is called bindu visphota, shukra sphota, or simply sphota. Sphota stretches out the point into space. Thus, the zero-dimensional nirguna Brahmn becomes the three-dimensional saguna Brahmn. Brahmn or space, is shuttled between zero-D and 3-D — that shuttling of Brahmn is both creation and dissolution. In zero-D the universe dissolves and in 3-D the universe re-emerges.

Because Brahmn is a 'shuttle-cock', it is also called atman. The word atman literally means one who shuttles — between the zero-D nirguna and the 3-D saguna. All that Brahmn contains is the distortions or disfigurations of that space itself. By distorting itself, space creates all. This disfiguration of space is called vivarta. Vivarta is the means of creation for Brahmn.

Since all that fall within space are its own vivarta or distortion/disfiguration, a God just cannot be there within space. Space has not and cannot have an outside; so space has not and cannot have boundaries. As space is the within and without of all, and all that are there in space are its own distortions, a God has no role in the whole round of being.

Therefore, Vedanta doesn't accept a God; hence, Vedanta is atheistic. If there is a God, if there has to be a God, that God is and must be space itself. For, space has no outside and all that are inside it are its own deformities. Space is the beginning and end of all. Space is the sole and Supreme Being. Space is the ultimate character or structure of all.

There is nothing other than space or Brahmn. Vedanta accepts space as the only possible God, and thus Vedanta is theistic as well. It is theism in atheism and atheism in theism.

One can make out Vedanta as being either theistic or atheistic in accordance with one's bent of mind but in itself, Vedanta is neither theistic nor atheistic. Vedanta is simply the science of the ultimate nature of being.

Dreamtime is about Deep Listening to Other Beats

By Narayani Ganesh

USTRALIAN Aboriginal creation stories have one common theme: that of a "Dreamtime". Australian folklore describes how the universe was created by ancestral beings whose activities in a primordial and featureless landscape resulted in the formation of the terrain and natural phenomena and the establishment of tribal law.

A K MacDougal, writing about myths of Australian Aborigines, describes how they considered themselves to be direct descendants of one or other of these mythological beings and so accept responsibility for that part of the country created by their ancestor. This is called the individual's "Dreaming" or "Totem" and lays on him a close personal link with everything in the environment. "There is no question in the Aborigine's mind of the unknown, unseen God of European man. The proof of the Aborigine's beliefs is to be seen in their natural world: its rocks, watercourses, trees and animals. This makes their belief a physically real and living thing, and their secular and ritual life reflects the immediacy of this belief."

When the eternal ancestors arose (from their slumber) in Dreamtime, they wandered the Earth, sometimes as animals — kangaroos, emus or lizards — and at other times in part-human, part-plant shapes. The Ungambikula — two beings self-created out of nothing — went about carving features and forms out of shapeless bundles they found lying near salt lakes and waterholes. In this manner, human beings got carved out of plants or animal shapes; hence, all individuals owe allegiance to animals and plants, reasons for their very existence.

Australian Dreamtime is the story of how the universe came to be, how human beings were created and how the Creator intended for humans to function within the cosmos. Myths talk of a seed power, and every meaningful activity, event, or life process that occurs at a particular place is believed to leave behind a vibrational residue in the earth.

Writes Robert Lawlor: "Plants leave an image of themselves as seeds. The shape of the land and its unseen vibrations echo the events that brought that place into creation. Everything in the natural world is a symbolic footprint of the metaphysical beings whose actions created our world. As with a seed, the potency of an earthly location is wedded to the memory of its origin. The Aborigines called this potency the Dreaming of a place, and this Dreaming constitutes the sacredness of the earth. Only in extraordinary states of consciousness can one be aware of, or attuned to, the inner dreaming of the Earth".

Interconnectedness of life forms is the web of life. Aboriginal wisdom emphasises the importance of learning to listen to a different beat. Indigenous knowledge is based on the levels of intimacy and engagement with other species on a daily basis. Deep listening is recommended for evolving friendly inter-species relationships. Good communication is as much the ability to listen as making oneself heard. By forging a complementary relationship with the environment, indigenous people learnt to co-evolve peacefully with other species of animals and plants.

Kindle the Spirit: Venerate Nature

By Indu Jain

TODAY, there is a worldwide movement to protect the environment. But this concern has been part of the Indian ethos since ages. The five basic elements — kshiti or soil, jal or water, panak or fire, gagan or sky or ether and sameer or air from which life has emerged — have all been objects of worship, forming an integral part of Indian tradition. The elements are deified, as they are believed to be protectors of jeevan tatva (life). But they can protect and bless us only if we give them due respect.

Love and respect for Nature is inherent in our culture; this is a unique feature of India's value system and philosophy. We regard our rivers as we would our own mother. We worship them. When we float a diya or lamp on the dancing waves of the holy Ganga, Yamuna or Kaveri, we are only paying tribute to them. Worshipping them is only an expression of our gratitude for all that they have given us. Our civilisation has flourished along river banks. These rivers have brought many of us closer to one another.

Rivers are symbols of patience. The great Ganga originating at Gangotri, journeys patiently to Kolkata. Quenching the thirst of the plains of northern India, the Ganga carries her blessings to millions. So holy is she that a mere dip in her waters cleanses us of all our sins.

Every drop of water is precious. This is evident from the following lines of the medieval Hindi poet Raheem: "Rahiman pani rakhiye, /bin pani sab soon /pani gaye na ubare, /moti manus ehoon."

The poet says that we must preserve every drop of water, for, a single drop saved inside the oyster's shell, forms a pearl. The word pani is also used to describe the grace and dignity of man. Thus, preserving pani is as essential as preserving one's own grace and dignity.

We revere Nature. Whether it is the Tulsi Chaura in our courtyard or the Batt tree which is believed to protect the marital bliss of a woman or the holy Peepal, all trees are considered to be equally important. Worshipping trees and relating them to our lives is a unique tradition. By teaching us to worship Nature, our great sages gave us the key to survive on earth.

Science today is trying to convince us how important vegetation is for our lives — something that our forefathers did centuries ago. Protection of forests is an important part of environmental concerns. Today, cleaning the waters of the Ganga is crucial to our existence. But, unless we enrich this duty with a sense of respect and devotion, we will be unable to succeed in this mission.

Our forefathers had understood the heart of the matter. They knew that only a sense of gratitude and an understanding of our interdependency will help us realise how much we owe to Mother Nature. Despite this ancient wisdom, we are yet to grasp the gravity of the situation.

So what we need today is to recreate this respectful attitude towards Nature. To reach this message to each individual — that the environment is not a dead object, but a living thing — should be our topmost priority. This is vital for our survival. Hence, the responsibility to save the Ganga from damage should be undertaken with a sense of gratitude and humility.

But this cannot be imposed on us; it has to come from within. We need to find a way to kindle this spirit within ourselves in order to make us fully aware of our responsibility to Nature. Only then will we understand that the Neem tree outside our home is much more than just a source of datun or nimodi. Neem purifies the air we breathe in, it is a source of healing. The ecological imbalance we observe today is the outcome of the ill-treatment we've meted out to Nature.

If only we stop this and show some sensitivity, she too, in turn, would shower her blessings on us. Our relationship with Mother Nature cannot be one-sided. Mother Earth has nurtured life in her lap. At the very least, we can save her anchal from further destruction and pollution by protecting the flora and fauna that gives us our life sustenance.

The various save-the-environment fronts, fora and organisations, which are trying to save the environment from further degradation today, will succeed in their efforts only when this is combined with a deep sense of respect for Nature. We have to believe that our survival depends on the survival of Nature. To protect the environment is to protect ourselves. This feeling must come from our inner self.

The scene today looks gloomy, but we should continue to nurture the hope to improve. As the poet says, "Khiza ka rang gehra ho chala hai har taraf, lekin/abhi ummeed baki hai, koi patta hara dhoonde." (Though the prospects for the environment are bleak, yet, there is hope that we'll find a green leaf somewhere...)

An Agnostic's View of Life and Death

By Khushwant Singh

THE one principle that should be at the core of any religious belief is ahimsa or non-violence: not to hurt any life, human or otherwise. Killing is not right. Killing animals to eat them is not a civilised thing to do, but carnivores exist in nature and in many places, humans have to subsist on non-vegetarian food for reasons beyond their control. But wherever possible, vegetarianism must be practised.

Hurting people physically or mentally, whether by word or action is wrong. Ahimsa is more important than prayer and kirtan. Ahimsa should be the central principle of your faith. But you have to raise your voice against injustice. Then, if you hurt someone who has hurt other people, it is justified. But the death penalty is barbaric — it is murder by the state.

Once, as editor of The Illustrated Weekly of India, I wrote an editorial on the issue of hunting and killing animals for sport. Then I sent individual letters to chief ministers of states asking them to ban shikar. Some of them responded by banning shikar. As one who has faith in ahimsa, I feel good about this.

So life should be lived with compassion and non-violence. I think a lot about life and the way we live it; I also think about death and how we deal with it. In fact, I'm writing a whole book about death. It's called Death at my Doorstep.

The basic point is, we don't know where we come from; we also don't know where we go after death. In between, we might know a little about life. People talk a lot about body and soul. I've never seen a soul, nor do I know anyone who has seen one. So for me, death is a full stop. I don't subscribe to the theory of rebirth endorsed by Hinduism and Buddhism nor do I believe in the Judeo-Christian belief in a Heaven and Hell. Ghalib said: "We know the truth about paradise but to beguile your mind is not a bad idea."

When I met H H The Dalai Lama, I told him I didn't believe in God. He threw his head back and laughed, saying, nor do Buddhists. I often wonder, how only Hindu and Buddhist children relate incidents from previous births while Muslim and Christian children don't?

There is nothing unique about death. Death comes to all who are born. So we don't need to pull a long face when death comes. Of course, it is human nature to grieve for someone you've lost. But that's no reason to create a big fuss, wailing and screaming. Nor is there any need to have elaborate rituals and kirtans.

Death is in the order of nature. When your time comes, die with dignity. I'm a member of the 'Die with Dignity' society formed by Minoo Masani 20 years ago. I can't say I don't fear death, but I'm more concerned about whether it is going to be a long-drawn-out painful process rather than worry about what happens later.

Iqbal wrote: "If you ask me about the sign of faith/ When death comes to him,/ he should have a smile on his face." I'm all for the ancient tradition of celebrating death. When people over 70 years die, their death should be marked with celebrations that include band music, dancing and feasting. It is a sign of maturity and acceptance of the inevitable.

I've discarded all religions but I feel closest to Jainism. Every person has the right to end his life, after having fulfilled his worldly duties and if he feels he has now become a burden on others. It is legitimate to want to extinguish your life.

Acharya Vinoba Bhave and Jain munis have done this. I wish to be buried with just a tree planted over my grave — no tombstone, nothing. If you live close to the sea, go for burial at sea. It saves wood.

Looking for the Soul in the Double Helix

By Deepak Chopra

F we secure a bit of Einstein's DNA and replicate it, will we be cloning Einstein's mind too? Nobody who believes in materialism has ever explained the soul as separate from mind. Jesus, Lao Tse or the Dalai Lama each must think, feel, and express his spiritual insights, all of which require a mind. DNA gives birth to cells, the brain is made of cells, which give birth to thoughts, and one category of thought is religion, which expresses the soul.

Hence, DNA is the source of the soul. The line of reasoning is enticing and disturbing in equal measures. If our DNA contains the "story of life", it has to contain the soul. Yet it seems impossible to declare that strings of chemicals spun onto a double helix could yield the spiritual richness of mankind. The base pairs of a gene are primitive, akin to simple sugars. I can mix a bag of cane sugar with assorted amino acids, dissolve them in salt water, and after a million years this chemical soup will not write a nursery rhyme, much less paint the Sistine Chapel or deliver the Sermon on the Mount. But if there is only one genome, doesn't it have to?

DNA is not just a sequence of primitive chemical bits. In between the bits are spaces, and it is the spacing, along with the sequences, that actually contains the information in the code of life. Fully 97 per cent of DNA is inert, serving no known purpose except to provide spacing. Gaps have a nice talent; they form patterns, and life is nothing if not an incredibly complex set of patterns, constantly shifting, overlapping.

So if God could be in the gaps, not in the chemicals, then what? A new concept of life emerges in which the arrangement of our genes is the real source of life. By analogy, the ineffable inspiration of a Hamlet cannot be detected by studying the ink on the first folio; the ink had to be arranged by Shakespeare in a unique way. So your DNA may encode every expression of your soul without actually being your soul.

To a triumphant geneticist, the invisible gap that separates the codons of DNA are trivial, no more than empty space. Yet quantum physics has already proved that emptiness, the void, is the womb of creation. Across the horizon of space-time is a place that is neither space nor time. Nothing exists there, not the slightest speck of matter or energy. Yet from this level of nature comes all intelligence, all creativity, indeed every possibility that could ever exist or even be imagined. Sounds an awful lot like God. Or the soul.

If you take a step back from DNA, isn't it obvious that it has a will of its own? The genome project is nothing but DNA discovering itself. Indeed, the impulse of a scientist to study genetics comes from DNA. So are we to suppose all this was a random sequence of events? Or in those invisible gaps, formed billions of years ago, did genetic chemicals contain the potential for an unseen future in which life would become fascinated with life?

The universe that created each of us is still inside us, in the form of encoded energy and information. The infinitesimal curlicues of DNA could be unwound, and written on it would be the history of the cosmos. Assuming that the Big Bang was just a fraction cooler or hotter, an entirely different universe would have been born. Now take the logic a step further.

The infinite fields of energy and intelligence that we all embody — the overall pattern that births all other patterns —must be the soul. A soul is pure creativity, pure intelligence, pure awareness. It transcends time and space by partaking of this moment and all moments, this place and all places. Why then does science stand so firmly as the sceptical gatekeeper who would deny us validation of our souls?

Ironically, science is separated from the soul by no more than the tissue of concept. And here is that concept, as enunciated by the contemporary philosopher Ken Wilbur: humans are unique in that we can see with the eyes of the flesh, the eyes of the mind, and the eyes of the soul. Science accepts the first two, but not the third. We will never know the secret of life until we see through the eyes of the soul, as do visionaries, artists, madmen, and saints. Their experience is just as valid as that obtained through a particle accelerator. We only have to look in the right direction.

How to Embark on an Incredible Journey

By Harmala Gupta

T is a truism that we are creatures of habit. Very soon what may have initially been a challenge becomes a routine and predictable affair. We seem, by and large, to prefer it that way. Every now and then, however, comes a challenge that requires a supreme effort of will to absorb and routinise it. A life-shattering experience is one such instance.

You are left with the shards of your life and have the task of rearranging the pieces. Instinctively, you want to recreate the past. But, like Humpty Dumpty, you find that this is an impossible task. A break has occurred and the only way forward is to accept it. It could even become a liberating experience for here is an opportunity to create what you will. You are no longer a prisoner of the past for you cannot take the future for granted.

Talking to people who have suffered a major loss, you find that this is exactly what they did. A friend said to me recently: "I am at peace as I am no longer in the race." What she meant was "the rat race". She is certainly very much part of the human race and more so than she has ever been. How many of us forget this and routinise our lives to the extent that we take each day for granted?

How many of us still feel thrilled to see the sun rise or set? If we dredge our memories, there must have been a time when we had once felt small and insignificant against the forces of nature. May be it was when we took our first steps and had to fight gravity to do so. How did we lose out on this feeling?

We lose our bearings when we begin to see the universe through eyes full of ambition and greed. Life lived this way is all about taking; there is nothing about giving back.

But "it is in giving that we receive". This is not about buying expensive gifts for family and friends or about giving alms. It is about giving of yourself — your time and your humanity. These are unquantifiable things and so, unfortunately, they are often disregarded.

It is also about allowing yourself to feel for the other in a way that leaves you feeling vulnerable and exposed. For it is only by doing this that you can help another. "If she could do it, and she is no super woman, so can I." This is the basis on which support groups around the world have provided hope and encouragement to people who have suffered terrible losses.

Often, the first reaction on hearing bad news is to immediately jump to the conclusion that the person involved must have deserved it. This is self-protection and a way of assuring oneself that it cannot happen to you. I have had so many people tell me that once they were diagnosed with cancer, they were forced to listen to accounts of people who had died miserably of the same illness. Once again, those who heard the news took refuge in the predictable. It is much too challenging to believe that a set course can be changed by an act of will.

This is exactly what people don't want to hear because it puts the onus for change squarely on their shoulders. However, for the person facing a situation of mammoth proportions, there really is no choice. It is a question of picking up the pieces and starting all over again or going down under.

This is where a return to one's child-like nature can make all the difference. It is not just about being positive, it is about seeing life as an adventure and rediscovering joy in little things. It is about daring to enter hitherto uncharted territory. It is about the thrill of the journey itself and no longer about reaching the destination.

Tiger Tells A Tale in Kargil's Shadow

By Jyotirmaya Sharma

WO stories appeared a few weeks ago in this paper. One was about the trauma of a tiger in war-ravaged Belgrade. The poor animal was so frightened by the bombing of Belgrade that he started chewing his own paws. The other story was a moving account of a man suffering from rabies. The man died a few days after the story appeared.

Eyebrows were raised at the timing of these stories. Why bother about a tiger in Belgrade or a man bitten by a dog when our soldiers were dying in Kargil? asked the sceptics. Does it not exhibit a degree of callousness towards our own people? they asked. Are the sceptics moved by the horrors of war — memories of dead sons, husbands, fathers and friends? Or is it the guilty feeling of being alive?

While the jawans and officers fighting in Kargil are truly brave and deserve our admiration and gratitude, every instance of war in the modern world raises a number of very difficult questions. An immediate reaction is that war traumatises all living beings and harms non-living entities. The tiger story, therefore, signifies the ultimate futility of all war as well as the sanctity of all life forms.

Amidst the war in the Mahabharata, Sri Krishna found time to nurse the wounds of the horses. The Jayadrathvadhaparva (13-16) vividly describes Krishna removing arrows from the bodies of the horses, massaging them and giving them food and drink: Krishna, adept at looking after horses, rid them of fatigue, nervousness and wounds. He removed the arrows from their bodies, massaged them and led them to drink water. He bathed them and fed them.

If defending our national borders is a supreme act of patriotism, improving the standard of living of ordinary citizens — giving them opportunities, security, a clean environment, corruption-free governance — should also be seen as a yardstick to measure patriotism. If the latter standard is applied, a majority of our political establishment could be branded unpatriotic.

Yet the very people who are invoking sentiments of patriotism and nationalism are responsible for bad governance and incompetence. When Duryodhana came each day of the war to seek Gandhari's blessings, all she said was that dharma, not adharma, should triumph. The tragedy of modern wars is that they are far removed from notions of righteousness. Today, citizens are required to commit themselves to a "total mobilisation" in the undefined interests of the State.

Young men and women die in order to pay for the follies of those who rule in their name. It is important that in times of crisis, people do not lose sight of the little things of life. Overwhelming emotions such as patriotism ought not to smother equally significant emotions such as truth, love, beauty, empathy and wisdom. Mars is always contrary to the Muses. Nero would never be forgiven for playing the fiddle while Rome burnt.

Wajid Ali Shah has been condemned as decadent because he wasn't interested in statecraft and let his kingdom slip into the hands of the British. While it is difficult to condone their actions as rulers who had failed to perform a particular role, they did contribute to other facets of life and culture.

Ernst Junger, that great aesthete of war, made the following entry in his diary during the Nazi occupation of Paris in 1943: "When all buildings shall be destroyed, language will nonetheless persist. It will be a magic castle with towers and battlements, with primeval vaults and passageways which none will ever search out. There, in deep galleries, oubliettes and mineshafts it will be possible to find habitation and be lost to the world." This is the ultimate expression of faith in the subtle, sublime and imperishable exemplified by language, which becomes the locus of survival. Wars in this century, by implication, do not produce an inner experience — no diaries, journals, poetry or novels spring from an experience of war.

It is, of course, impossible to visualise an incomparable Vedantic text like the Gita emerging out of a modern-day battle situation. Civilisation, then, is not about single agendas, homogenising instincts, totalising ideologies and designer emotions. Like life itself, civilisation manifests itself best in diversity and plurality.

As Stendhal said, civilisation consists in "combining the most delicate pleasures... with the frequent presence of danger". If this truth is forgotten, the individual pays for it with his life, but if it is a nation, it pays with its history.

Do not Waste the Gift of Human Life

By Parmarthi Raina

RI Adi Shankaracharya says in his 'Vivekachudamani': "Three things are difficult to obtain, and if obtained, it may be taken as due to the grace of the Divine: human birth, desire for liberation and guidance and protection of a spiritually enlightened person."

Most people believe in the existence of God, and also in the presence of a soul (atma) in every living entity. Yet not many consider it necessary to inquire into and understand the nature of God or of the soul. They pay perfunctory obeisance to God and occasionally seek mundane material favours from Him. They are quite content to go through life, with its fleeting pleasures and not-so-fleeting miseries, simply fulfilling the four activities common to all species of life: eating, sleeping, mating and defending. Finally, time (kala) overtakes them and they succumb to death, without having realised the true value of human life.

There are two sides to human life: the material, which concerns the body, the mind and material nature; and the spiritual, which concerns the soul and God and the relationship between the two.

A majority of people spend their entire lives catering only to the needs of the body and mind. The most compelling of these needs is to please the senses (kama), for which one needs wealth (artha). To obtain sufficient wealth, many are persuaded to procure it by any means, fair or foul. Vedanta does not deny man the enjoyment of sense pleasures or the necessity of earning money. In fact, Vedanta accepts man's requirement for both and has included them in the four purusharthas (pursuits or objectives) prescribed for him: dharma (code of values), artha (wealth) kama (sense pleasures) and moksa (liberation).

Vedanta, however, cautions us not to chase kama and artha indiscriminately and recommends that these two pursuits are tempered by dharma. Dharma is thus placed before kama and artha as it regulates the two. These three purusharthas are called trivarga and they serve man's material quests.

Moksa, the fourth pursuit, is separate from the trivarga, because it is a spiritual quest. For moksa, knowledge and realisation of the soul is a prerequisite. Sadly, however, we completely neglect the obligation to understand the soul. Although several questions plague our minds, we do not try and search for answers. What is the nature of God? And of the soul? What is the relationship between the two? What happens after death? How does the soul transmigrate from one body to another? Are there heaven and hell? What is the purpose of life?

Vedanta holds that human birth is rare and, therefore, precious and it should not be wasted. The Srimad Bhagavatam states, "Having obtained, after many births and deaths, this rare human body, though ephemeral, affords one the opportunity to attain the highest perfection (liberation from samsara, the perennial cycle of birth and death). Thus, the wise and heroic human being should earnestly strive for the ultimate perfection of life before death overtakes him. After all, sense pleasures are available even through the bodies of other life species."

Man is graced with a unique nature. He is distinct from and far superior to all other life forms. He is endowed with a highly developed consciousness (chaitna) and abundant intelligence coupled with the ability to discriminate (buddhi). Vedanta considers the discriminate faculty in the human being, when not under the sway of his sensory urges, to be truly unique. But man fails to manifest his unique nature because the animal tendencies (pasu bhava) in him are overpowering. If he can subjugate these tendencies, his real nature, humanness (manusya bhava), will come forth and his spiritual awareness will start to grow. He should, therefore, not waste this precious human body, which is the highest form of life among the 8.4 million species and, instead, use its unique nature to inquire into and discover the higher spiritual dimensions of life.

The rarity and usefulness of the human body is once again highlighted, this time by Lord Krishna Himself, during His last discourse with His friend and devotee, Udhava, in the Srimad Bhagavatam. "The human body is rare and available by one's good fortune. It is a most suitably built ship, which, when captained by a competent guru and favoured by the wind of God's grace can be used to cross the ocean of samsara. If a man fails to utilise all these favourable conditions, he should be called a killer of his own spiritual self."

God of All Things, Big and Small

By Irani Mukharjee

LL creatures, big and small, are beautiful creations of God. Very often, however, we tend to either ignore the 'small' or exploit them for selfish reasons. This is where religion and spirituality can help restore to us a holistic perspective so that all of God's creations are given due respect.

Religious thought and spirituality serve a larger purpose only when they find positive expression in action. Theory without implementation is of no use. I fear that the concepts of religion and spirituality are being hijacked by humans for their own selfish purposes, leaving out all the other, equally if not more, valid forms of life.

When we say 'all', it should include all forms of life. All animals are created by God. But only one self-styled animal, the human being, has arrogated to itself the right to pray to the Creator. Is this true spirituality?

All animals enjoy the right to maintain a relation with their Maker, for all life forms are created by the Almighty with the same five principal ingredients, popularly referred to in Indian tradition as the panchbhoot. Any kind of social ostracism towards animals is an insult to the Creator. Yet, even places of worship are being tainted with the blood of 'lesser' life forms.

In many instances, animals are admitted into the inner precincts of a place of worship only in order to be sacrificed at the altar. It is unfair for one animal to sacrifice another to propitiate the gods, when all are God's creations.

The Buddhist principle of ahimsa or non-violence which was an integral part of our culture began to be forgotten with the decline of the Pala dynasty of Bengal. Mahatma Gandhi's efforts to inculcate in people respect for all forms of life did make a difference, but only for some time.

Superstition encourages disrespect for animals. Sacrifice, pelting stones and other forms of violent treatment being meted out to them are all justified in the name of ritualistic religion. The natural rights of animals are being replaced by the 'naturalised' right of the human being who excludes other species from human made roads and places of worship.

We have no qualms about pronouncing generalisations when it comes to animal behaviour. If a few dogs are infected with rabies, all dogs are viewed with suspicion.

An encounter with one ferocious dog makes us brand all dogs as being ferocious. But we don't do this to humans, do we? If a few men commit murder, are all men branded as murderers and punished?

True spirituality should inculcate love of all life forms in humans. There are several tales in Hindu mythology which talk of the combined effort of humans and other animals to attain a designated goal. The Ramayana narrates the ceaseless effort of the monkey king to restore peace. Most Hindu deities are associated with various animals. The Indus Valley deity, Pashupati, remains a historical fact.

In the verse, Ma Nishada, Valmiki curses the hunter who killed one of a pair of love birds. All existence is complementary; we all coexist on the planet. All life forms share available resources. We should not misuse the 'survival of the fittest' theory to marginalise and oppress other life forms.

As human beings, we need to be mindful of the welfare of other animals, too. No religion would condone cruelty to animals. No spiritually evolved person would encourage the killing of old, unproductive or infirm animals. Indeed, we need to act in compassion and love when relating with one another — but the same attitude should be extended to animals as well.

Don't Get Trapped By Your Emotions

By Rohini Singh Chopra

AVE you ever wondered why you sometimes feel low, drained, energyless? You might feel so after a stressful period — because of trying circumstances, a spell of hectic work or sudden trauma. Often, you are unable to pinpoint a reason for it. And for some of us, it may have become a state of being; a joyless, purposeless existence.

Each of us has been given the gift of life fuelled by the life-force or prana. Why does this precious resource dwindle, sometimes to desperately low levels? Take a look at the following energy-guzzlers:

1. Worry: For many of us this is as natural an activity as eating or sleeping. We worry about things that we are convinced are doomed to happen: that those who are ill will not recover; others who aren't, will fall ill; bad times will remain bad; good ones will take a turn for the worse; children who are in school will not get admission into good universities; those who have might not do justice to the opportunity given to them; bright children of marriageable age will not find good alliances; and of course potential good candidates might turn out to be not-so-good.

In fact, as a worrier can tell you with conviction, nothing in life is certain so there is much to worry about. It is responsible to worry. There is always ample fuel for the fire of worry. And this is a greedy, unsatisfied fire, always ready to devour more. It is a vicious story of burnout. What does this mean in energy terms? Consider this: energy follows thought; so as you continue to feed that fire — as you think negative thoughts about all the things that may not turn out as well as you wish, you are actually giving energy to those very occurrences that you wish to avoid. As you continue to obsessively think about them and imagine the consequences, energy continues to flow to them. Often you find them manifesting, little realising your role in their creation. Soon you feel drained, unhappy, low in energy.

2. Resentment: If worry drains you with fears of the future, then hurt, resentment and regret keep you chained to the past. As you nourish memories of people who have hurt you or let you down, of circumstances that have betrayed your expectations, or of unfulfilled dreams, you are only draining energy to something that is in fact dead and gone.

Think about it: somebody said something hurtful to you years ago. You can still remember and talk about it with tears in your eyes. That person, meanwhile, is no longer a part of your life; he may even have passed on, but you continue to leak energy to this thought. No wonder you wake up feeling life is unfair and joyless; a burden rather than a gift.

3. Guilt: This is one of the heaviest emotions that wears you down as you continue to carry it. We all make mistakes, feel regret or remorse over situations in our lives; commit acts of omission or commission. But we cannot let go; we believe it would be irresponsible to forgive. So we continue to internally condemn and scold, instead of learning from the fall and getting up to move on. It is much like climbing a mountain with a heavy trunk tied to your back. How can you really look around and enjoy the view?

Is all this just glib talk? Can we really decide not to worry for the future or let go of our disappointments of the past easily? Can we just as simply forgive others and ourselves? Can I be emotionally free to decide?

Good Thoughts, Words, Deeds and More

By Ervad Marzban Hathiram

ACH and every creation of the supreme Lord Ahura Mazda has been given a specific divine task, to be performed at various stages of existence. Yet, caught in the whirlwind of daily life, we tend to forget our responsibilities, distracted by worldly pursuits.

Our actions spurred by our weaknesses take us even further away from God, deadening the mind to the ultimate goal, salvation. How should we concentrate on our spiritual responsibilities without losing track of our secular liabilities?

The Zoroastrian scriptures offer the solution in following the practice of Meher-Patet. Meher signifies absolute truth, and Patet, the practice of immediate and public acceptance of a wrongdoing. How does this help? Meher is also the Yazata or divine entity connected with the sun's rays. The rays of the sun engulf the entire earth and every atom of our body craves for the life-giving properties of the sun. When we follow the practice of Meher-Patet, the life force of Meher present in the sun's rays is infused into our body and alerts our consciousness towards spiritual responsibilities. Thus roused, we become open to Meher Yazata.

Meher Yazata sows the seeds of goodness in us, enriching our soul with physical, mental and spiritual wellness, enabling us to reap the fruits of our hard work. We become aware that our deeds must not be just those driven by our personal needs, but should rise to the level of Hvarshta or good deeds which fulfil the divine task entrusted to us by our maker.

Once we convert our deeds to Hvarshta, we become associates of nature, attempting to help other entities in their divine tasks. As we understand more and more of the mysterious working of nature, we realise the magnitude of the task entrusted to us. We observe the working of the Celestial Ones and decide to sing their praise. We get more conscious of what and how we speak, ultimately speaking less and praising the work of the divine ones through the Mantras.

By controlling our tongue, we are able to advance to the level of Hukhta or good words — that is, words which when spoken have the effect of immediately delivering what they promise.

As we attain the stage of Hukhta, we come into direct contact with the Divine. We realise that all of creation works according to the Ahuna Vairya: The Divine Thought and Will of Ahura Mazda. Our entire mind becomes focused on how to further the Will of the Creator. We realise the futility of harbouring other thoughts and, hence, begins the process of cleansing our mind and thought process.

After long practice and Divine help, we gain control of the mind, removing all extraneous thoughts from it, replacing them with just one central and overarching thought: 'How shall I further the Will of Ahura Mazda?' As our mind gets cleansed, it becomes the abode of Vohu Mana: the Good Enlightened Mind, and our thoughts transcend the temporal and attain the state of Humata or Good Thoughts.

This is the real meaning of the oft-quoted phrase Humata, Hukhta and Hvarshta, used to describe the so-called adage of the Zoroastrian religion: good thoughts, good words and good deeds.

Since our current thoughts, words and deeds are far from reaching that state of perfection, we need to adopt the path shown by Prophet Zarathushtra: cultivating the habit of truthfulness at all times, and developing the moral courage to publicly accept our failure when we get diverted from this difficult practice.

Ways To Overcome Stress

By Sant Rajinder Singh Ji

INCE the time when man experienced the first flicker of self-awakening, his attention has remained focused on problems of worldly existence. No sooner is one problem solved, a new one springs up, thereby creating stress and tension in the mind. A disturbed mental state can lead to stress-related illnesses and so we need to find an acceptable way of preventing mental, emotional and physical effects of stress.

People often turn to meditation as a way to overcome emotional and mental strain. Meditation helps us withdraw our attention from the outer world and focus it at a point between and behind our eyebrows, thereby stimulating, what is called, the 'third eye'. By focusing our attention on it, we can reach higher levels of consciousness.

For meditation to work, the first step is to find a time and place in which we will be least distracted by our environment. For this, the time between three and six o'clock in the morning is ideal. However, we can meditate any time when we will not be disturbed. We should sit in meditation at times when we are fully awake.

The second step is to sit in a pose most convenient to us. We can sit on a chair, on the floor or on a sofa, either cross-legged or with our legs stretched out. One can even meditate standing up or lying down. The main thing is to meditate wherever and however we feel comfortable. Whatever pose we choose, we should be able to remain still for a long period of time.

The third step is to sit in concentration. Once we pick a pose, we should close our eyes gently and concentrate on what lies in front of us. This should be done without putting pressure on the eyes. Initially, there is darkness. Then with the inner eye we should gaze lovingly into whatever is in front of us. We should be relaxed but attentive.

The fourth step is silencing of thoughts. Once we focus our attention, the mind will present distractions in the form of thoughts. One way of stilling the mind is to repeat any name of

God with which we feel comfortable.

The fifth step is concentrating on inner light or sound. To concentrate on inner light, slowly repeat the five syllables taught during initiation by the master. While mental repetition goes on, sit quietly and lovingly gaze into the centre of whatever is lying before you.

As we meditate more, we will be able to see inner vistas. The second practice of meditation is listening to the inner sound. We concentrate our attention and listen to the inner sound current. Once we are tuned in to the divine melody, we can travel on the sound current to higher realms of consciousness.

Meditation is a way to connect with divine power. We might feel permeated with a feeling of love which engulfs and fulfils us. We experience a profound peace and bliss unlike any we can find in this world. The meditation process helps us at two levels. First, it relaxes us physically. Second, it puts us in a state where we are absorbed in bliss and become oblivious to problems of the outer world.

By meditating on the inner light and sound, we are placed in contact with the radiant energy coming from realms that lie beyond the physical world. There is a powerful current of divine love, consciousness and bliss. Meditation does not literally eliminate problems of life, but gives us a new perspective. We become detached from suffering because we are able to find a spiritual anchor. Through meditation not only can we learn the art of living, which helps us overcome life's stresses and strains, but also discover a way to experience the Divine.

Yoga of the Vision of the Cosmic Form

By Gautam Jain

HE Bhagavad Gita is a scientific text dealing with the knowledge of life and living. This knowledge consists of the eternal principles governing human existence. These principles remain as relevant today as when they were expressed thousands of years ago on the battlefield of Kurukshetra. Arjuna was a prince and decorated warrior of those times. However, when confronted with a personal challenge on the battlefield, he succumbed to the pressure of the situation and became incapacitated; he was beset with doubt, and he could not act.

Arjuna represents today's human being. The battlefield of Kurukshetra is symbolic of the world, with the numerous challenges it presents. In spite of being well educated and proficient in our respective fields of activity, we succumb eventually to the stress and strain of life when faced with challenges.

The reason for this paradox is that the education we receive is woefully inadequate in helping us deal with life itself. It only provides us with the information necessary to work in a particular field of our choice. But living is a skill, a technique. One needs to learn and practise it just as to be a good sportsman or musician involves regular practice and perseverance.

Yet, very few of us look at the act of living as a skill. As a result, we remain stunted, with an extremely narrow vision limited to our petty, mundane existence and its innumerable worries and anxieties. We end up missing the larger picture. Steeped in ignorance, we continue to live, oblivious to the purpose for which we exist.

The eleventh chapter of the Gita is titled, The Yoga of the Vision of the Cosmic Form. The cosmic form is presented before Arjuna as a gigantic figure of Krishna, the form that is symbolic of the

Underlying Reality that supports the manifested universe. "Arjuna, behold as concentrated within this body of Mine the entire creation consisting of both animate and inanimate beings, and whatever else you desire to see. But surely you cannot see Me with these human eyes of yours; therefore, I vouchsafe to you the divine eye. With this you behold My divine power of Yoga" (XI.7, 8).

Krishna explains to Arjuna that he ought to understand that Reality and not get carried away by the passing phenomena of names and forms that he perceives in the everyday world.

This universe is governed by an essential Law that holds its functioning together. We must try to understand the functioning of that law and our role in it. Without knowledge of these fundamental issues, we become confused and deluded in life. And then we succumb to the pressures of various challenges.

Krishna then expounds the knowledge to Arjuna in detail. He explains to him the functioning of the cosmos and his role in it. As a kshatriya, his duty is to fight with a higher vision. He should re-establish righteousness in a country battered by the immorality and barbarity of the Kauravas. In the process, he should not worry about the results that would accrue to him.

Armed with this knowledge, Arjuna regained the intellectual clarity he had lost and became composed. He cast aside his mental weakness and emerged with a firm vision of his duty in life. He was able to overcome his enemies and emerge successful.

We too can be successful, armed with this knowledge, in gaining the vision of life's mission, and acquire the mental stamina necessary to discharge our duties and responsibilities in life. We can then live fulfilling, meaningful lives.

The Path Through Difficult Times

By Vikas Malkani

LIFE often takes unexpected turns. It's a universal truth that grief and pain spare no one. And when they arrive, the resultant emotional trauma can last for months, even years. Betrayals, infidelity, deception — from those we trust and care about — can never be planned for, or anticipated.

Yet, these very traumatic experiences are also life's turning points. The experience or the happening itself is not as important as your perception of it. The way you cope with what has happened is what makes the difference.

When such events occur, your minds and hearts become inundated with feelings of loss, helplessness and a sense of being defeated. If left unresolved, those traumatic experiences may suppress the body's inbuilt immune system, and leave you more vulnerable to illness and disease.

However, no incident or situation, no matter how bad it may look in its first moments, is final or fatal. No personal trauma or emotional setback is insurmountable. To overcome such a sudden and intense personal hurdle requires patience, understanding and, above all, an awareness that looks beyond the immediate to the larger picture.

Spiritually, all our problems and setbacks are merely lessons for us from life, acted out through people, events and places, and leading to our self-evolution. There are no full stops in life, only commas. And the sooner we learn our lessons, the faster our life moves forward in a more harmonious manner.

There are certain steps that can be followed to make the path through the mental and emotional turbulence of a personal crisis smoother. First, accept the pain, and the mistakes and errors on your part. To prepare yourself mentally to meet the demands of stressful circumstances, you need to accept that your life has temporarily been turned upside down by the unforeseen traumatic event, and believe that opportunities for self-growth and lessons exist within the new circumstances.

Also believe that you can learn your lessons and grow to be a

51

better, happier and more aware individual. Secondly, accept that the healing of grief and pain is a process that takes time. Each person experiences pain differently and reacts to different stimuli in different ways. But certain emotions felt as a result of a sudden traumatic event are common.

Denial, anger, fear and symptoms of depression such as sleep problems, loss of appetite, and difficulty in accomplishing daily tasks are stages that we all pass through. It's important to recognise that the mourning or recovering process takes time. Sometimes, it takes many months or more to pass through.

Thirdly, seek periods of solace and draw help from family and loved ones. Identify what feels best to you for finding solace during times of grief. Spending time close to nature, or browsing through old letters and photos are all valid options.

The key is to do whatever allows you to express your grief and pain, instead of bottling it within. Above all, spend time with your loved ones. Researchers have repeatedly demonstrated a vital link between the strength of our social support systems and our emotional and physical resilience under severe personal stress.

Finally, work towards resolution of conflicts and issues. Usually, the reasons for our grief and pain are of our own making even though we cannot clearly see this while experiencing the trauma. The reasons for the crisis are possibly the results of our choices and/or decisions.

Remember, denial of the reasons cannot lead to healing or resolution. A clear understanding of the reasons, followed by acceptance, and a firm commitment for positive change is the answer. Prayer and meditation are very helpful tools to tide over a personal crisis; they bring stability and allow inner cleansing.

A broken heart, if that's what you face, being emotional trauma, requires much more care than a broken bone or any other physical ailment. Here are some practical tips to heal a broken heart. First the do's. Do stay calm and treat yourself gently. Do recognise and accept your injury. Do stay with the pain, do not deny it. Do take time to heal. Do accept comfort from family and loved ones. Do take care in making important decisions, and attempt to resolve the conflict.

And now the don'ts. Don't panic. Don't deny the hurt, or the mistakes. Don't dwell on the negatives, or stay isolated. Don't make choices, or decisions that create more chaos and pain. Don't fall into relationships on the rebound. Don't be afraid to admit your mistakes, or to ask for help. Above all, don't lose faith.

Stay Fit With Quantum Yoga

By Neelam Verma

HE individual physical body we are identified with is our action body, the microcosm or vyashti. It has to adopt itself to the environment outside that is the macrocosm or samashti.

In the cosmos, nothing exists in isolation. Everything is related to every other thing, which means that relationships are spontaneous and instantaneous. All dimensions of the microcosm are in a state of rhythmic balance, within and without. This association forms the fabric of the cosmic supernet or mayajaal where everything is in a relative but dynamic equilibrium. It is as though the entire cosmos is projected in the human body, while the human body, in turn, is projected in the cosmos. The dynamic connections are made through breath, senses and electromagnetic radiations. The individual action-body is gifted with a vital feedback not only within itself but also with the cosmic Self.

Quantum yoga is the realisation of the vibrational unison of the cosmic Self with our inner self. This vibrational chemistry harmonises the infinite cosmic energy with our vital life energy and generates the rhythm of life in our inert organic body. Healing is an integral part of this rhythm and is active every moment of our life, with every breath we take. The Bhagavad Gita defines our mortal physical body as kshetra that is governed by an eternal force, the kshetrayna.

How does the kshetra get its positive and negative qualities and how do they affect the perceptive brilliance of kshetrayna? The body is created out of a mixture of physical elements. Perception of ego in this kshetra gives it a specific identity. Wisdom is then kindled with the supreme mantra of intelligence. This kshetra is endowed with a range of emotional expressions. The senses have been sanctified for perceptive and reactive functions. A variety of good and bad qualities come to dwell in this kshetra and threaten its balance.

The wheel of kshetra derives its energy quotient and functional guidelines from kshetrayna. In ignorance, we allow our ego to generate dark clouds of desires and cravings around our consciousness. Our body, mind and heart then fail to get the energy quotient. We fall sick easily. This is the 'quantum of descent'. We get easily irritated and become temperamentally unstable. We become vulnerable to stress, anxiety and anger.

Anger triggers intellectual disintegration. According to the Gita, this 'fall' is inevitable; so we need the spirit of a warrior to take up the heroic challenge of controlling our mind. A disciplined mind becomes our best friend. Let loose, it becomes our worst enemy. As the sublime glow of kshetrayna pervades our body, mind and heart, our process of downfall is reversed and we enter into a 'quantum of ascent'.

Slowly, the mind gains in strength. Our intellect and intuitive judgement improve. We become better adapted to resolve conflicts. We acquire patience and contentment. This is the ultimate essence of quantum yoga. With patience and contentment, work efficiency improves. Our inner vision gets magnified and a metaphysical transformation takes place at the core of our heart.

With this our consciousness becomes ritambhara. It begins to deflect egocentric desires and comes to rest in the crystal clear brilliance of the pure and peaceful inner self. In this state of perfect alignment, our body starts radiating a sublime aura, which annihilates all sickness, suffering and disease. We look not only healthy but also beautiful. This timeless and boundless beauty is the hallmark of a person who is happy and peaceful in a blissful state of sthithaprajna. When we achieve this state, even the atmosphere around us gets changed with the sacred vibration of quantum yoga.

Young and Dejected?
Here's Some Cheer

By M P K Kutty

IFE in society today is becoming increasingly more competitive. This is also reflected in the educational system, where admission to select courses has become almost impossible.

During admission time, university campuses are normally buzzing with activity. There is excitement and tension in the air. The human quest for power, prestige and wealth is visible in the student-aspirants.

The courses that offer the best career opportunities are most sought after. For, a good career means a comfortable life. Career counsellors on campuses guide and help young students make right choices, taking into account their aptitudes and inclinations. Despite the counselling, most students prefer to opt for only those courses and subjects which hold the promise of a bright future. Their ultimate goal is the 'good life'.

There are others, who, for various reasons, do not seek to study further. Many choose to enter their parents' vocation. This is the trend in families engaged in trading, business, crafts, cultivation and, increasingly, in politics. But there is something that is common to both categories of seekers: they have dreams of a happy future.

However, there's a catch. Not all student-aspirants will get the course of their choice. There are bound to be disappointments since the demand for seats is much more than the availability. But setbacks and lamentations are not the preserve of disappointed students. Some of those who get to realise their ambitions are equally disillusioned.

We cry over what we lose. Often, we also cry over what we gain. Two little teardrops were floating down the river of life. One teardrop asked the other: "Who are you?" It answered: "I was shed by a girl who oved a man and lost him. And who are you?" Replied the first teardrop: "Well, I was shed by the girl who got him."

King Solomon, one of the wisest men who ever lived, wrote an account of his experiences and his efforts to find satisfaction and fulfilment in his life. He records: "I undertook great projects. I built houses for myself and planted vineyards. I made gardens and parks and planted all kinds of fruit trees in them...I bought male and female slaves...I also owned more herds and flocks than anyone in Jerusalem before me. I amassed silver and gold for myself... I became greater by far than anyone in Jerusalem before me." Yet, in the end, when he surveyed all his possessions and achievements, he concluded that they represented nothing more than his vanity.

King Solomon then made a deliberate effort to acquire wisdom. However, he soon discovered that although wisdom is desirable, the same fate overtakes the wise man and the fool. He realised that everyone shares a common destiny. He then looked for meaning in the happenings and strivings of men "under the sun and found that even those few wise men who searched for the meaning of existence — while claiming to have understood — did not comprehend it truly".

King Solomon also found that the swiftest man did not always win the race; the strongest man did not always win the battle; and wealth did not necessarily accrue to men of wisdom. It was all largely a matter of chance. Success or good fortune does not always go to those who deserve it. So if you are a disappointed student who failed to get admitted to the course of your choice, don't be disheartened. You might not realise your dreams of becoming a doctor or an engineer, but that doesn't mean that you are unfit for any other profession or vocation.

Whatever your field of work, take interest in it. Work diligently to the best of your ability. Take pride in your work.

Mantra for Happiness — Loving Detachment

By Amitava Basu

IMPLY put, happiness is satisfaction of mind. However, different individuals have different perceptions of how to achieve happiness. For some, happiness lies in wealth; for others, it is in rank and position; yet others find happiness in fame and name. Commonly, happiness is measured by achievement in terms of money, property, other material possessions, power, name, fame, education, lifestyle, position and social status.

In the quest for 'happiness' individuals tread a path that destroys the inner good instincts and virtues. Craving for material wealth begets greed and greed leads to corruption. Similar is the outcome when passion for power drives one's mind.

Life is not permanent; nothing in life can last forever. Saints and sages have realised this truth and lived away from pursuit of mundane objects and worldliness. But ordinary people fail to see this truth. Maya impels individuals to believe that material achievement is the truth of life; and, in the process, it fuels attachment to worldly pursuits and sensory pleasures.

Growing attachment breeds addiction to material attainments. In turn, such addiction intoxicates the human mind, making it oblivious to the truth. So real happiness remains a mirage. Mahasiddha Naropa, the tenth century mahasiddha of the Kagya School of Tibetan Buddhism, was born in a rich and powerful family.

He renounced his family and wealth at the age of 25 to be ordained as a monk-scholar in Nalanda University where he became a leading scholar and respected faculty member. He later left in search of a guru to attain moksha and found Tilopa, who was one of the four mahasiddhas of India.

Once Tilopa handed a string full of knots to Naropa and asked him to untie them. Naropa did so and gave the string back to

Tilopa. Tilopa threw the string away and asked Naropa what he understood. Naropa replied that all beings are tied by worldly attachments and they need to untie themselves.

Dispassion for attachment to material pleasures and comforts restrains one's desires, dispels worries and fears and guides us to the path of peace and tranquillity. To be dispassionate, you need to search your heart everyday and practise untying your passion for mundane matters. An individual who meticulously endeavours to get rid of expectations, hopes and fears can set the mind at rest and reach a stage of detachment from worldly pleasures.

This, however, cannot be achieved overnight. This change needs preparation of the mind and takes time. It is a practice that an individual needs to pursue for "being in the world but not of it". You should have a mind open to everything but attached to nothing. This does not mean that you have to run away from your family, society, duties and responsibilities and be less sensitive. One needs to recognise the Divine in others and work to serve the Divine.

Some may argue that the incentive behind every work is gain, without which an individual will not be motivated to work. Then how will the detachment happen? The gain is realisation of what is Eternal and the alleviation of material suffering following from this realisation.

Sri Guru Granth Sahib says: "As the lotus flower floats unaffected in the water, so should one remain detached in one's own household." The lotus flower is not tainted by the slime in which it grows. It is an attitude that an individual needs to develop through belief and practice; and only this can emancipate one from worldly attachments to derive pure happiness.

Discover the Secret of
Happiness Within

By Deepak Nigam

N life everyone ceaselessly acts pursuing various goals. In and through all such pursuits one is ultimately seeking nothing but happiness. But are we clear about what happiness is, where to seek it and how to achieve it? Real happiness is an equanimous state of mind, when thoughts are at rest. It is a state of cessation of agitations, which are caused by unfulfilled desires of the mind. Desire is the thick stream of indiscriminate thought which flow in you, drawn towards the world of objects and beings. You entertain desires within to fill the void or overcome the sense of unfulfilment you feel within you.

To quieten these agitations caused by unfulfilled desires, we go through a variety of experiences at the physical, mental and intellectual levels of our personality. We contact objects, beings, emotions and thoughts of the world and try to find fulfilment in them, e.g. a child with toys, youth with wealth and physical pleasures, the elderly in a newspaper and old friends.

If our desires are fulfilled, we are happy and if not, we are in sorrow. But as George Bernard Shaw said, "Man has to face two tragedies in life, one when his desire is fulfilled and the other when it is not." In both cases he ultimately faces mental agitation, in one case it's early and in the other it's later.

The world is in a constant flux of change. The experiences of this world are passing and fleeting. And the happiness derived from the world of objects, emotions and thoughts is also passing in nature. For example, joy derived from an ice cream lasts only for a while. When you read a book or newspaper, it absorbs you only for a few hours.

So worldly happiness is not permanent. Therefore, lacking the knowledge of true happiness and its source, one focuses on the world to provide us with true happiness. But that results in experiencing instant joys followed by emptiness, sorrow and suffering. A young man plucked a beautiful rose to enjoy its fragrance. When he brought the rose in contact with his nose to enjoy its fragrance, a bee inside the rose suddenly stung him on the tip of his nose.

The man cried in pain and the rose fell from his hand. In reality, there is not a rose of 'sensual pleasure' that does not have the bee of 'injury' concealed in it. Indiscriminate pursuit of pleasure objects invariably comes up against the law of neutralisation. It is the state where any further contact with the objects gives no more happiness, whereas its absence creates sorrow.

A person in the midst of riches and plenty may remain dull and bored, yet the absence of these would generate sorrow. A regular alcoholic in contact with alcohol gets no pleasure but abstinence from it brings him suffering.

True happiness, we should realise, does not belong to the realm of the physical, emotional or intellectual levels of our personality. It belongs to our true nature. Beyond the levels of our body, mind and intellect lies our Real Self, our supreme nature, the source of infinite happiness, the Godhead in us. Christ said, "The kingdom of heaven lies within you. He who knoweth shall find it." And Guru Nanak said the same thing: "If you want permanent happiness, seek the Ram within you."

We don't have access to the Godhead within because it is veiled by our desires. In order to unveil our Real Self, Vedanta says that one must raise oneself above desires. As long as one functions on desires, they multiply, which causes further mental agitation and stress. Instead, with the help of the intellect, one must channelise these desires to a higher ideal, towards an unselfish cause in life.

Desires must neither be suppressed nor indulged in. Through discriminative control and channelising, they get sublimated. As desires drop within us, there is increasing peace and happiness within our being.

Vedanta provides us with the knowledge of life and living, the mental equipment to tackle life's problems, to always be happy and remain unaffected by sorrow. As one gets more and more subjective happiness, the less one is dependent on the external world for happiness. This everlasting happiness which lies right within the core of our heart, we search in vain in our outward experiences.

An old lady lost her needle in her cottage. It being dark inside, she went out under the street lamp to search for it. So it is the case with most of us. We search externally while the kingdom of heaven lies right within us. Discover it. That is the secret of happiness.

Look Beyond Peace and Violence

By T S Sreenivasa Raghavan

OT a day passes without a reference to the need for peace. Still, the booming guns don't fall silent. While peace is discussed because of its absence, war is the subject of debate on account of its ever-menacing presence. So we need to find answers to two important questions: can we achieve lasting peace? Can we shed individual and collective acts of violence? To find convincing answers, we will have to analyse peace and violence in their totality, both from the point of view of individuals and communities.

Atma-shanti is peace within and a soul that is peace-less within can hardly be peaceful outside. The Ribhu Gita is an exposition of advaita by the sage Ribhu to Nidagha, in the Siva-rahasya. Ribhu, in fact, holds the individual responsible for everything that is good or bad; and also for everything that is neither good nor bad.

For, what exists is only Brahmn, the eternal state of Supreme Consciousness.

Ribhu says to Nidagha: "I'm of the nature of all activity/ I'm of the nature of the doer of all/ I'm the protector of all/ I'm of the nature of the destroyer of all/ I'm ever the nature that is not anything/ I'm of the nature that is established as myself/ I'm ever of the nature of the undivided Absolute/ Inquire steadfastly into this every day" (14:8).

One could, however, argue that violence is a part of human nature while peace is not...because, the six innate, intertwined, yet pivotal qualities of humankind are desire, anger, greed, delusion, ego and competition. Shanti (peace) is absent whereas its anti-thesis krodha (anger) is conspicuous by its presence.

Ribhu deals with this question too when he says to Nidagha: "There's nothing to be discarded as disagreeable/ Nothing to be added as agreeable/ There's neither a master/ Nor any disciple/ There's nothing called knowledge/ Knower or the knowable/ There's no sentience/ Or mindless insentience/ Nothing auspicious/ Or inauspicious for me/ I'm the difference-less Brahmn" (8:20).

By pronouncing that there's nothing to be cherished as agreeable or discarded as disagreeable, Ribhu — the prophet of non-duality — opens our eyes to the fact that everything has to be accepted in its totality: peace and violence, happiness and sorrow, ego and simplicity, natural and unnatural; because their denial or suppression will result in confrontation (10:3).

Our real challenge lies in going beyond discrimination. If we talk about love suppressing hatred, we'd get only a love that's coated with hatred. If we talk about God suppressing the Devil, we'll get only a Devilish God. And, if we talk about peace suppressing violence, we'll get only a violent state of peace.

Like peace and violence, everything in the world is highly individualistic. If you insist that you'll change only when the whole world does, it'll never happen. Ribhu expresses it better: "Nidagha! As there's nothing apart from your Self/ Consider your Self as yourself/ Experience your Self, and ever enjoy/ The bliss of your Self in yourself/ Become peaceful and immersed/ In an ocean of happiness/ Without any of the least sorrow/ Remain my son as a mass of bliss!"

Neither peace can put the violence down nor violence can mutilate the face of peace. We have to learn to accept...without attachment or detachment. A supreme state of consciousness alone can achieve this. Then we'll discover the harmony that lies beyond peace, beyond violence. But we have to begin with the self. That's why J Krishnamurthi said: "You are the world!"

Peace or Violence, Make Your Choice

By Satya Pal Singh

ECHNOLOGICALLY, we live in a borderless world. In reality, however, we exist in compartments, separated by walls of caste, religion and geography. We acknowledge the information explosion as being a great achievement and take pride in describing ourselves as a knowledge-based society.

Snowed under as we are with mounds of information, we are facing a paradox; we find that ignorance levels are growing as well. The rate at which we are accumulating information is not commensurate with the rate at which our awareness is growing.

How much more do we know about reality and existence? The amassing of worldly 'knowledge' is acting like a moat that prevents the passage of an even more important kind of knowledge, knowledge about the Self. The ignorance of Self is compounding individual tensions, creating discord in relationships and is responsible for changing the character of the family as a reliable support system.

More and more people are acting out of fear, hatred and violence. These negative emotions have pervaded almost all spheres of life, whether in relationships or societal activities. Since long the basic objective of all human beings is to attain happiness and peace. Towards achieving this goal, all schools of Indian philosophy advocate the cultivation of the art of discovering the Self.

Sage Narada tells Sanatkumar in the Chandogya Upanishad: "...Only he who knows the Self, goes beyond sorrow". By knowing the Self, the unseen becomes the seen, the unknown becomes the known and all doubts get destroyed. But to know the Self, we have to shake off the falsehood in us and recognise illusion for what it is. This is the way to dissolve all differences between individuals, communities and faiths.

Values are relative, as is reflected in the following story: A Brahmin priest was returning home after taking his customary dip in the sacred waters of the Godavari river. He was chanting mantras as he pushed the beads on the rosary to keep count. On reaching the main road, he noticed a donkey lying dead, apparently the victim of a motor accident.

Deeply disturbed by the sight he remarked: "The killer of this innocent animal will surely go to hell." While he was cursing thus, someone came up from behind and tapped his shoulder. He informed the priest: "The donkey has been killed by your own son." The Brahmin replied: "Actually, the animal is relieved from the chain of life and death and the person who facilitated this will surely go to heaven." Looking for peace without making any effort to look for the Self is like searching for footprints of birds in the sky. The process to see the Self is simple but requires practice and perseverance.

First, we need to believe that our goal in life includes achieving happiness, peace and bliss. Second, we need to spare at least 10-15 minutes every day, morning and evening, to reflect on what effect any action or word of ours is going to have on other people—are we helping them feel better or worse? Third, we get sensitised to the way we affect other fellow humans. Fourth, we need to attune ourselves to receive or hear the truth.

Only critical analysis, manna, and nidhi dhayasana or daily practice, can take us towards truth. I would like to end by quoting Heraclitus: "If man craves for gold, he must dig for it or be content with straw. If one wants pearls, one has to dive deep into the sea or be content with pebbles on the shore." The choice is ours: whether we want enduring peace and brotherhood or perennial strife and violence.

Peace is Life, War is Death

By Firoz Bakht Ahmed

T was said of Prophet Mohammed that God wanted him to be an example of how to live peacefully among others like a simple man, to nurture a family, to work for a living and to accept equally the joys and sorrows of life. But there are some who, while professing loyalty to Islam, are actually doing more harm than good. For instance, Osama bin Laden's brand of "Islamic jehad" is utterly un-Islamic and goes against all tenets of Islam.

In Islam, taking an innocent life is equated to killing the whole of humanity. Osama is not a true Muslim. He is not even a jehadi as jehad is waged not against non-Muslims but against ignorance and suppression. Osama and his ilk have done more harm to Islam than any of the other so-called enemies of Islam. The very meaning of Islam is to submit and never to offend.

The Prophet abhorred war that crippled and maimed people both in body and mind and believed that the aim of all people irrespective of the religions they follow, is to coexist in a manner that mutually benefits everyone. All countries should collectively shun violence and war. We should strive to follow what Mahatma Gandhi, the apostle of ahimsa, entreated all human beings to follow: the principle of non-violence.

In Mahatma Gandhi and His Apostles, Ved Mehta writes that once during the communal riots in Noakhali, Bengal, Gandhi said that the country had become clearly divided between two expressions of religion. The choice for us is between the 'religion' of terrorism and true religion that has always advocated peace, communal harmony and mutual coexistence. True religion propagates compassion, fellow feeling, selflessness and self-transformation.

Regarding the call of "Do or die!" Gandhi interpreted the slogan thus: its true essence has nothing to do with aggression of any sort. "Do here means Hindus and Mussulmans should learn to live together in peace and amity. Otherwise I should die in the attempt," suggested Gandhi. When someone asked Gandhi his views on war, his reply was just one word: ahimsa.

Ahimsa for Gandhi was not merely a negative state of harmlessness but a positive state of love, of doing good even to the evil-doer. He believed that in a war, there is no victor, only losers. Those who propagate war don't know really what war means today. If they did, they wouldn't propagate war. Even more than the millions who will surely die an instant death, life for survivors would only mean something worse than even death, in the aftermath of a nuclear detonation that would leave behind a lingering and harmful radioactivity.

A nuclear exchange, even the most 'controlled' one, would devastate entire regions. In such a war, there can be no victor. Today's nuclear weapons contain a lethal potential that will make even the atom-bombed Hiroshima and Nagasaki appear to be mere shadows.

How should we get ourselves out of this combat mode? First, we must try and clear our minds of all clutter. Next, we should cultivate a positive attitude so that we can face any kind of confrontation with a composure and patience that is absolutely necessary to rein in whipped up passions. Only then can we generate solutions that are reasonable and peaceful.

Gandhi stressed that it was wrong to be obsessed with battles and their results. He was anguished by the brutal riots during Partition. He said: "Without ahimsa there is neither Pakistan nor Hindustan; only slavery awaits both the nations torn asunder by mutual strife and engrossed in barbarity."

For every conflict there is always an amicable and concordant solution. War is not a solution as with its seemingly territorial victory, it rather exacerbates the hardships of the peoples of the countries at war. Peace is life. War is death.

Compassion and Peace Go Hand-in-Hand

By Hwasun Yangil Park

UDDHISM advocates tolerance; to accept that there are differences in human experiences; that diversity is part of life, whether in experiences, cultural backgrounds or religions and faiths. Buddhism is the religion of compassion, mercy and forgiveness for all life forms. It does not preach the superiority of its belief systems over those of other religions, nor does it believe in any sort of hierarchical ordering of faith systems; it does not discriminate against anyone, least of all on account of faith or belief.

The recognition and embracement of diversity and pluralism and the resulting absence of any coercive or violent means for proselytising is the very essence of the humanism of Buddhism. All life forms are treated as sentient beings of equal status, possessing innate dignity and potential for achieving Buddhahood. Remember, we are all brothers and sisters who eventually share the fruits of all our actions in an increasingly globalised world community.

Buddhism teaches us to practise pacific behaviour and actions in everyday life to achieve the goal of true non-violence, love and collaboration. It is first and foremost practice, not scholarship. Those who recite sutras and mantras faithfully but neglect engaging in practice may, in fact, betray the true spirit of Buddhism. All Buddhas of the past practised in the human realm, and their greatness showed in their behavioural manifestations.

Throughout many lives, the Buddhas practised generosity, befriended all, suffered with all, and worked ceaselessly to alleviate suffering among all life forms. The Sakyamuni Buddha taught a great many sutras and mantras and practised them in person for 49 years after his enlightenment. He taught and set the example for kings, ministers, farmers, men and women, children and people of all faiths.

In this way, he engaged in social actions and established the tradition of humanistic Buddhism to purify people's minds and to help establish a 'pure land'. All Buddhas were role models in establishing everyday practice of compassion and peaceful collaboration. In order to emulate the Buddhas, we should first discover and cultivate our own Buddha-nature, intrinsic dignity and the Bodhi mind, and the door to our ultimate freedom from worldly suffering.

By discovering and cultivating this boundless treasure and resource, we can also help all other sentient beings rediscover their kindness, pure and boundless compassion, joy, equanimity, humility and gratitude, all of which they already possess. Several small steps can be taken to make a beginning to help us find our true nature. Treasure life, your own and of others; show gratitude; respect nature; be aware of national resources; do not be greedy; be content.

We need to recognise our traditional responses to disorder and chaos. We tend to punish those individuals who are responsible for such disorders to serve as a deterrent to further aggravation. Punishment, however, can produce only temporary results. To transform violence to harmony, jealousy to praise, greed to generosity and impurities to purity, we must not rely on negative and reactive punishments.

We must promote, in a proactive manner, mutual understanding and respect, compassion, collaboration and honest transactions among all people. The same principles of mutual understanding via continuing dialogues, practice of concessions and international redistribution and aid systems need to be applied in the arena of international politics and economics. This will help reduce conflicts among different ethnic, national and religious groups.

Way of Peace: Love as Antidote to War

By Deepak Chopra

AHATMA Gandhi offered a startling truth: "There is no way to peace. Peace is the way." To countries bogged down in the morass of war, this revelation could be a beacon of hope.

The history of peace movements in the US has been divisive and bitter. Thirty years after the Vietnam peace movement sputtered out, it is still considered political suicide for a presidential candidate to actually promote peace.

Senator Kerry, who has an anti-war background, is desperately trying to disguise that fact. President Bush, who has a background of shirking war, is just as desperately trying to cloak that fact by being a hawk...

Both candidates have failed to offer peace as an option, since they agree on a central tenet, that war is the way to peace (if not this particular war against Iraq then a general war on terrorism). Such a viewpoint, if carried out, can only lead to more violence. Gandhi was correct when he pointed out that lasting peace is achieved only when a nation realises that peace is the way, in and of itself.

But what would that way be? The way of peace can only succeed by providing substitutes for all the satisfactions that war brings. Officially, we deplore war as a nation, but beneath the surface it is clear that war is satisfying.

First of all, war is a habit that we are comfortable with. Like any other habit, we can reach for it the way a chain-smoker reaches for a cigarette, even while muttering that we have to quit.

In Mira Nair's film adaptation of Vanity Fair, a woman comments smugly at a party, "War is good for men. It's like turning over the soil." So war, it seems, provides an outlet for male aggression...

Can a political candidate begin to talk about the satisfactions of peace? These were real enough before 9/11, although we took them for granted. In peace one breathes easily. There is space to allow for bonding and connections with other people. Arguments proceed with mutual respect for either side.

Gandhi went further to show that the way of peace ends suffering and oppression, not by warring against an enemy but by bearing witness to wrongs and allowing sympathy and common humanity to do their patient work. Nelson Mandela and Mother Teresa lived different aspects of peace, which was proven to be a viable way to achieve great things.

When an individual is exposed to the way of peace, reality changes down to the very cells in the body. An experimenter who showed random subjects a movie of Mother Teresa found that their immune systems responded immediately. The rise of an immunoglobulin called IGA proved that exposure to love actually increased the body's defences.

This happened regardless of whether the subjects approved of Mother Teresa or not. It's time to be honest with ourselves. We have not given the way of peace a fair chance. The way of peace requires a genuine commitment to everything that is the opposite of war. Gandhi's most cherished value was ahimsa, which is much more than simply non-violence.

Ahimsa is reverence for life and a vision of human beings put here on this earth to explore their spiritual birthright, excluding no one, making no one your enemy. The way of peace can lead to nobility of soul. The way of war, as we are learning with sinking hearts, can only lead to the grim degradation of our most cherished values.

Waging Peace with an Awakened Mind

By Ajahn Sumedho

WAR is not real. It is caused by ignorance of our true nature, which is peace. To realise this, it is important to meditate. Meditation brings one into an awakened state where one is able to get in touch with the still point within. Doing this might seem unimportant from the society's perspective, which lays great emphasis on winning wars and making money.

To the unawakened mind, life seems like a reiteration of problems. This is because it sees problems as being caused by external conditions. The US might see Saddam Hussein as the root of all problems, and vice versa. This is because the mind is caught in the trap of right versus wrong, good versus evil. The US might say that Iraq must be in a certain way, anything else is unacceptable. This happens when one does not realise that the reality and karma of the present moment is not the ideal. It just is.

Meditation opens us to the present. We learn to operate from an intuitive wisdom rather than an intelligence that insists on examining external objects so that we gloss over our true nature by identifying with this and that. By forming immutable ideals, we use them to despise ourselves. The reason people have problems with themselves is because they aren't what they think they should be. Life can be only what it is at that point. Yet so much of our energies are spent forming goals or ruing past failures. Being physically in the present but not being open to it creates suffering.

What do we mean by 'peace'? If we are unaware of our true nature, peace can become boring. So many times, peace is available to us but we ignore it, preferring to excite ourselves with TV, shopping or something else. Don't take this to mean that the Buddha was a critic of the world. He just wanted us to live in it mindfully, to recognise its reality.

The mind is conditioned to be forever caught in doubt and uncertainty, so much so that it resists giving them up in meditation. The fear is of losing control; it is what we call 'the dark night of the soul'. It is the point when the sense of being secure in ideals, conventions and dogmas needs to be dropped. This is a stage of growth and needs to be recognised as such.

As we begin to trust intuitively, we learn to let go. Letting go of grasping leads to an insight into our true nature, peace. That brings the realisation that war is something we create. Even if someone is persecuting us, by examining the situation, we realise that it is our own mind that creates the feeling of suffering.

When I began meditating, I would try to control my thoughts and get rid of the ones that seemed 'bad'. The more I resisted and tried to get rid of them, the more power they seemed to have. The states that I was trying to 'get over' emerged even more forcefully during meditation. Then I realised that I wasn't being asked to destroy, only to see. The more I received my anger without reacting to it, the more it ceased. And when anger ceases, what remains? Peace.

Consciousness is not a culturally conditioned phenomenon. It begins at birth and is experienced through our bodies. When we are born, we don't see ourselves as Buddhist/Christian, male/female, and so on. We acquire perceptions of ourselves later. If we judge another culture, it is through values of our own culture, which are relative. Consciousness is what remains when there are no attachments of any kind.

Consciousness is not cultural, it is the point where we all merge. That is the only way out of this crisis.

Give Peace a Chance: Don't Go to War

By Prem Rawat

WARS happen when intolerance reaches epic proportions, when the reasons for war become greater than the sanctity of peace. Wars happen when we fail to realise the value of being alive. World leaders try to bring peace, but it is not an issue of institutions. It is human beings who start wars. Before a war begins outside, it starts inside.

The war on the inside is more dangerous because it is a fire that may never be put out. Wars are being fought because peace is not being found within, because it is not being allowed to unfold.

We are all searching for something, we may call it success, peace, love, or tranquillity. It is the same thing. What we are looking for has many names because we do not know what we need.

To find what we need, we look around us. To know where to find what we are looking for, we first need to ask ourselves where we can find it. Have we considered looking within?

Living is not an easy task, especially if we want the best of it. We have to mine for it. Mining is not easy. We have to take out what we need and leave the rest. If we want to mine for peace, we have to seek what is precious and discard what is not. The thing that we are searching for is not outside of us. It is within us. It always has been and always will be.

Contentment feels good, and it is not an accident. It is not an accident that peace feels good. Peace is already here, and it resides in the hearts of all human beings. Peace is something that has to be felt. One of the most incredible powers we have is that we can feel. When we place peace in front of that power to feel, we feel peace. We are here to be filled with gratitude, love and understanding. We carry a lamp within so bright that even in the darkest night, it can fill our world with light.

This light is waiting to be found. Peace makes no distinctions. It

73

does not care if we are rich, if we are poor, or which religion we belong to. It does not care which country we live in. Peace is waiting to be found. Waiting to once again feel whole, not separated by all the issues that divide our lives. Peace is when the heart is no longer in duality, when the struggle within has been resolved.

When peace comes to the heart, serenity follows. Love comes flooding in, uncontrolled. Joy cannot be held back. It bursts through because it is right. That is peace. Peace needs to be felt, love needs to be felt, truth needs to be felt. As long as we are alive, the yearning to feel good, to feel joy, will always be there, and as long as it is there, there will be a need for it to be discovered.

Life is a journey. We are passengers in a train called life, and we are alive in the moment called now. The journey of life is so beautiful that it needs no destination. On this journey, we have been given a compass. The compass is the thirst to be fulfilled. The true journey of life begins the day we begin to seek to quench our thirst. This quest is the most noble one.

For many centuries, a voice has been calling out: "What you are looking for is within you. Your truth is within you, your peace is within you, your joy is within you." In our hearts, peace is like a seed waiting in the desert to grow, to blossom. When we allow this seed to blossom inside, then peace is possible outside. We have to give peace a chance. Will we give peace a chance?

Find Peace Through Awareness of Self

By Prasoon Pant

F we look around us today, we will find a world that is shattered by war and terrorism, the effects of which, if not in a direct manner, continue to influence us. The fundamental question on the mind today is: in what way can peace be achieved in the world to put an end to this suffering?

Some centuries ago, human beings were still conscious enough to pay heed to the spiritual side of their growth. In India, most people are proud of being a part of a spiritual legacy, which goes back to beyond Vedic times. The emergence of industrial and consumerist societies throughout the world brought along with it a new wave of thought and ideology: of wealth and the means for its acquisition.

Today at the pinnacle of the world's industrial and material glory, we see that there is neither an end in sight to poverty nor any contentment in those who have been a part of this growth. In fact, the new society, based on the ideology of wealth, and an ever-widening gap between the rich and the poor, is one of the root causes of war and terrorism that are plaguing us.

The rise of religious fanaticism in many parts of the world shows our failure in understanding the real meaning of religion, which is 'peace', and is the fundamental premise of all religions.

Then, what is the way to achieve peace of mind in today's times? It is necessary for us to find our place in the scheme of things, in this universe. The Buddha said that all life is a transitory phenomenon. He said, "Life is like a flash of lightning." We have such a short life that it is useless to waste it fighting each other and dissipating our energies in only acquiring material possessions.

It is of great value to follow a path of self-inquiry to attain peace and achieve happiness. When we begin the process of self-inquiry, we have to put our whole being into it. In us, viveka or conscience is the power to discriminate between right and wrong and can be said to be a spark of the divine element in us. The first process of this self-inquiry then is to observe one's thoughts, desires and feelings and to be 'aware' of them. This awareness is necessary and it might take time for a person to get accustomed to, as our mind is conditioned to, identify with our thoughts and emotions. The Buddha said that the mind can be a great obstacle in the path of realisation and, at the same time, it can be a great vehicle on the way towards enlightenment.

Once a person is aware of what goes on in his mind, he can proceed to deal with the thoughts and emotions that make a person cling to suffering of all kinds.

The second part of the path to self-inquiry is to root out the thoughts, feelings and desires that obstruct the path of self-realisation. All fears, anxieties, depression, anger and other negative feelings that a person experiences can be got rid off in this way. This is perhaps the most difficult task in the world, but to accept this challenge and to face one's weaknesses is worth the effort. In fact, it is at the core of all spiritual teachings in the world.

As we progress into this path of self-inquiry, we can pursue the practice of silencing our mind through meditation or concentration on some object like a deity, a symbol or even a material object. We can also concentrate on some higher feeling like karuna or compassion, and this is a very good way to meditate. The Mahayana or Greater Vehicle school of Buddhism describes karuna as an essential characteristic of a Bodhisattva or one who seeks nirvana or enlightenment not only for himself but for every living being.

The main feature of this compassion is that one thinks of alleviating the suffering of other sentient beings and wishes for their liberation before entering into Nirvana oneself. By practising this path of self-inquiry, one can gradually develop stillness of mind and there comes a time when we feel peace within ourselves. Then we can think and act in a calmer way, and without inner conflict.

Human life is full of ups and downs. What holds true in a person's life today might not hold good for tomorrow. We need to lead a life where finding peace within us should not only be the aim, but a necessary precondition upon which all other foundations of life can be laid.

Let's Build a Temple to Tolerance

By Swami Agnivesh & Rev Valson Thampu

N the name of God we ask you, the bloodthirsty actors in the tragedy of India, to have done with it. You have had your day. And you have played your hellish part to perfection. The land is littered with too many corpses already. Columns of smoke from fires of hate choke the air. The sun hides its face from this shame. Stars have fled from our sky.

The wails of widows and the shrieks of burning children mock the meaning of our national anthem. A thousand wounds bleed. Our hearts bleed. Mother India bleeds. The obscene stench of blood fills her nostrils. Enough is enough. Stop this abomination. For God's sake, stop it. Live, and let live. Live in peace.

God cries over the karmic debt mounting over this punyabhoomi. Life belongs to God. Like the rest of us, haven't you heard grandmothers say, life is divine? God is the Giver of life. He alone can take it back. By killing in the name of mandir and masjid, you make a mockery of both. On your lips, the name of God is a scandal. Your zeal is blasphemy. Can't you see this?

Your mandir-masjid, the monument of your mutual malice, silhouettes a tomb for God. Think not that He will look at it; for a thousand namaazes and yagnas cannot fool Him. He knows you not. Have you forgotten His words: "Let him be my greatest bhakta but if he injures a single fellow human being all his offerings I reject. His offerings will be not as made into a homa-kundam but like oblations offered to ashes."

You've incensed God with the cries of innocents. Justice belongs to God and He will uphold it. Think, is God blind? No, He sees. Presume God is deaf? Go and despair, He hears. The cries of babes pierce his ears. Burning bodies singe His mind. Are not those blanched in the grip of terror — Hindus, Muslims, all — His babes? Rest assured, the asuras and kafirs of injustice will have to pay: their backs broken by a crushing karmic debt that generations cannot expiate.

Oh, stop this sacrilege, the murder of our mutual trust. With that killed in cold blood in the darkness of your noon, what are we left with? Knives under sleeves? Poison in our wells? Anthrax in our entrails? Shall we then creep in stealth, watching each step, lest we are blown to smithereens, unawares? What are you achieving in the name of God? A jungle of spite and death where boys roar and range like beasts?

Won't you stop this desecration of religion? We don't know what to call it: you get us all so confused. Didn't you hear a child ask the other day: do their gods have fangs? Do they bite? Drink blood? Eat human flesh? Are houses the pipes they smoke after banquets of bloody brawls? You men of petty gods, children plead, won't you tell us why your gods have hearts of stone? Why has compassion fled from men?

They say you want to fight this war of gods to the finish. And see which god wins, and who loses. Who cares? Your gods are below our notice. India is the loser. And we care. What shall it profit us: this victory of vanity that sets fire to our sacred home? The global village laughs over this cat-and-mouse game. Let us, for God's sake, be better than a nation of cats and mice.

Go, give up: this pettiness. We demand: we, the people. A billion people. It is our house that you've set on fire! Weren't you brothers before you chose to go mad? Won't you be brothers again when sanity returns? When the earth quaked under your feet, didn't terror melt all hearts alike? Did death and destitution have religions then? Weren't you one in spirit when nature roared and revealed your cowardice? Wherefrom this cheap courage to kill, rape and loot under license? Is this not worse than the old cowardice?

Weren't you all neighbours? Who has turned you into killers? Do not tell us it is Ram or Rahim. Try first to erase the footprints of Ravan and Satan from the streets of your hate.

Come, all you stand by and watch this immolation. Shed torrential tears and douse this fire. Let not Bharat Mata burn alive while we have a tear to shed. Yesterday was a nightmare. Let it go. Let today be a new beginning: a shared dream. Let us rise and build together; for we do have a temple to build: the temple of India where God delights to dwell as love.

Fight Off The Devil Within You

By J L Gupta

UMAN beings belong to mother Earth. You are born here and you learn to survive on this planet, but you harbour the illusion that you have conquered everything. A human being feels proud that he has scaled high peaks and fathomed the depth of oceans. With the modern inventions, we are able to fly like birds, swim faster than fish and remain alive under water.

Man has even walked on the surface of the moon. But as human beings, we are not at peace, neither with ourselves nor with the world around us. In fact, we are under tremendous stress. We are struggling with our inner selves at all times. If we look at our lives, we find that we are virtually at war with the world around us.

On the one hand we talk about globalisation and aim at a borderless world. On the other, we worry about petty, personal gains. The only solution to this problem is that we need to work towards changing our mindsets. The Buddha had said that a human being can be free from the cycle of birth and death by the 'renunciation of desire'.

Human desires can be fought and got rid off. We can, by repeated practice, bring our mind under control and can attain the state of liberation from the negative thoughts and emotions of our being. However, to be liberated from these thoughts and desires, one must be aware of them first. By this method, misery can be put to an end, and real happiness can be attained.

The world is becoming a dangerous place to live in, and this is despite our claims of being civilised, of having evolved from the primitive to modern man and from the cave man to cultured being.

Many reasons can be attributed to this. A man longs to be the king of all kingdoms, but is too extravagant and idle. He desires that his writ should run through the whole world. But then he is lazy and lethargic. Man is mean, far inferior to other species. We are more human than humane. We have negative qualities such as anger, ego, envy, greed, hatred and jealousy, that we should consider overcoming.

We have allowed these qualities to become our consuming passions. We think that we are mightier than most. We think we are capable of destroying anything by using our might more effectively than mythological demons, about whom we have read in our childhood. Today, we have acquired weapons of mass destruction, which are capable of obliterating all life from the face of this planet.

As men we arm men. Then we destroy people without arms. All this leaves us with the inevitable feeling of sorrow. Then why are we giving vent to our anger? We let our wrath take over our senses. And we trust that it shall never burn us. We fight to satisfy our egos. The overpowering obsession of a man with himself motivates him to grab everything and to fulfil his greed.

Today, wealth alone is the God of man. The malice in our mind never misses the mark. We fight to primarily prove our power. We pray every morning when we wake up. But after that, we look for a prey throughout the day. It is also true that every prayer that an Indian raises ends with an invocation to peace. 'Om Shanti, Shanti' which means, 'God! Let there be peace. Peace everywhere.' Then why do we cry for war?

We need to be calm so as to be able to command. We must wage a war against anger, against hunger and illiteracy. We must realise that rancour can never be rewarding. We must learn to rein in the feelings of revenge. We must learn to be content. 'Riches' is not a bad word and poverty is not a curse. A person can be rich or poor, and his friends might be few, but, they would not be jealous of him, if they learn to be content with their own condition.

To be happy, we must learn to forget ourselves. We should resolve to wage a war against the devils hidden within. We should discover the God within us and learn to make peace with the world. We should spread joy amongst our fellow beings. This ought to be our resolution: to satisfy the sinews of our soul.

A Fervent Plea for Compassion and Love

By Mata Amritanandamayi

CONTENTMENT is within reach for a person who is compassionate and loving. The greedy, however, remain unsatisfied as they are constantly looking for bigger and better ways to fulfil their desires. At which point will they be satisfied — when they get a bigger house, a better car, higher designation?

To overcome this vicious circle, we need to replace lower thoughts with noble ones. A greedy person pays no attention to the quality of his words and deeds. Always fixing his gaze on the future, trying to figure out how to do this or that, he will spend his whole life planning, calculating, and dreaming. Unable to be in the present and enjoy what is right in front of him, he cannot relish even his food, because while he is eating lunch, he is planning his supper.

How can such a person be happy and content? The past and future are mere illusion. The past is dead and gone, and the future is yet to come. The present alone is real. If you water the branches of a tree, the water will be wasted. For nourishment to reach the entire tree, its roots have to be watered. So when we pray for humankind, we will also be benefited.

Unfortunately, our hearts are closed; we are loath to share. We are unable to rise above personal gain. Blindness of the eyes is bearable and can be managed to a certain extent. You can still live as a human being. You can still have a loving and compassionate heart. But when you are blinded by the ego, you are completely blind. Don't let your power and position, your name and reputation, your wealth and possessions make you look down on others.

If someone who needs help approaches you, you should smile warmly at him, have a compassionate word for him and listen. Even if you do not give him anything, smile and console him with loving words. You should be able to tell him: "Brother, I understand your problems. I know you are having a hard time. I wish I could help you. Unfortunately, I am not in a position to do so. Please forgive me." These words will have a soothing effect on him. They will act as balm for his aching heart. He will be consoled and think: "At least he gave me some comfort with his kind words. It is a great relief to know that good-hearted people like him still exist in the world."

He will feel enthused instead of feeling desperate and depressed. He will not think of committing suicide. Do not give up your wealth. Do not give up your expectations in life. Have them, but try to be compassionate. Try to feel the suffering of others. You are not a machine. You are a human being. You represent the human race.

Try to be loving and compassionate, because those are the signs of an evolved life. Remember, only a human being can develop compassion and empathise with others. You might think: "If he is suffering, it is his karma." It is none of your business to think about his karma. If it is his karma to suffer, consider it your karma to help him. Only helping others will help you evolve.

The ability to grow in love and compassion has almost been forgotten. By not making use of this rare gift, you are rejecting God, going against God and denying His gift. This is the worst thing that can happen to you. If something goes wrong in your work, that can be corrected. Material loss is not irreversible. But if you reject God's gift, that is irreparable. He wants you to use it properly. If you reject it, you are obstructing the flow of His Grace. You are building a barrier between Him and you. Your ego is the barrier.

Forgive and Inhale the Fragrance of Flowers

By T G L Iyer

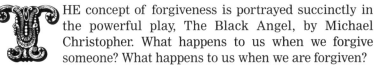HE concept of forgiveness is portrayed succinctly in the powerful play, The Black Angel, by Michael Christopher. What happens to us when we forgive someone? What happens to us when we are forgiven?

Christopher's play is about a former German army general, Engel, who tried to make a new life for himself and his wife outside a little French village. He had been imprisoned for 30 years, sentenced by the Nuremberg war crimes court. He hoped that people would forget and forgive the terrible past. He built a log cabin in the nearby mountains. He wanted to start anew.

A French journalist, Morrieu, could not forget the past. His family was massacred by the general's army. There was not a single survivor in the village. For 30 years Morrieu had planned his revenge. He said to himself: "If the Nuremberg court could not sentence General Engel to die, I will pronounce his death sentence and execute it." He stoked the embers of hatred and fear in the minds of the village radicals and revolutionaries.

They conspired to burn down the cabin at night, killing Engel and his wife. Morrieu, as a journalist, had several questions for the general: Why did he do it? After 30 years in prison, what did he feel now? So, he proceeded to the cabin, surprised the general and his wife and spent the whole afternoon probing his past actions, trying to analyse and learn the reasons for the tragedy.

He found the general full of regret and repentance. He was actually waiting to download his guilt to someone he could trust. Moved, Morrieu offered to smuggle the general and his wife to safety. He disclosed to them that the villagers would attack his cabin at night and kill both of them.

The general said: "We will accompany you only on one condition; that you forgive me." Morrieu could not forgive the general. He could save him, but forgive him, never! That night the villagers burnt down the cabin and shot Engel and his wife dead. The play when staged left the audience gasping for an answer.

Why was it so difficult for the journalist to forgive and why was it so important to Engel that he be forgiven? What is it that the general wanted which the journalist could not give? The Bible (I John 1:9) says: "If we confess our sins, He is faithful and just and will forgive our sins."

To forgive is not to forget. Forgetting is not hard. All you need is a bad memory or to treat the incident as insignificant. But to forgive is to make a new beginning, to start all over again with the person who caused you pain. It does not take away the hurt nor does it erase the past injury. It merely ceases to obstruct the path of a new beginning.

To forgive, you don't have to aggravate the guilt and squeeze the soul of the person. By forgiving, you can walk together into the future. In the Bhagavad Gita (chapter 12), Krishna describes 35 qualities of a devotee; one of them is a forgiving nature. Learn to forgive. Having forgiven another, what really happens?

The rancour, anger within, which was eating the vitals, is automatically washed and cleaned. It purifies the system. You become 24 carat gold, soft, solid and shining. Mark Twain captures this quality when he writes: "Forgiveness is the fragrance the violet releases as the foot crushes it." Spictetus said 2,000 years ago: "It is not he who gives abuse that affronts, but the view that we take of it. Your hurt comes from not what others do to you, but from what you choose to do with their actions. If you change your attitude about the hurt, you will soon find your victim status eliminated."

Forgiveness Helps Contain Anger

By Firoz Bakht Ahmed

E always look for the healing touch after someone has hurt, humiliated or insulted us. Samuel Johnson in "The Rambler" writes that a wise man will make haste to forgive because he knows the true value of time, and will not suffer it to pass away in unnecessary pain. On the other hand, anger is a short-lived madness; when a man grows angry, his reason rides out.

Fury and anger carry the mind away. True, anger is never without reason, but seldom is it backed by a good one. By controlling the anger of a minute, one may avoid the remorse of a lifetime. The Lord's prayer says: "Forgive us our trespasses, as we forgive those who trespass against us." He that forgives first, wins laurels. Surely, forgiveness is better than revenge. A Latin saying advises, "Forgive others often, yourself never!" If it is easy to get angry, it is difficult to forgive. He who holds back the rolling chariot of anger as it gathers speed, is a real driver while others are just holding the reins. "Thou hast the advantage of the angry when thou keepest silence." A man is outside himself when angry. If a man has anger in his heart, what further enemy need he fear? In the Book of Wisdom, Ben Sira quotes, "Lose not thy temper because of a scorner so that he use thy mouth as a trap. Anger breeds hate; forgiveness nourishes love."

Saying the words, "I forgive you" could be the most powerful thing we could ever do. Forgiving doesn't mean giving in. It means to let go. Once we forgive, we are no longer emotionally handcuffed to the person who hurt us. One reason is that it compensates for the powerlessness we experienced when we were hurt. We may feel more in charge when we are filled with anger.

But forgiving instils a much greater sense of power. When we forgive, we reclaim our power to choose. It does not matter whether or not someone deserves forgiveness. Shakespeare wrote in Coriolanus: "Anger's my meat; I sup upon myself!" To be angry is to invite the faults of others upon ourselves. Rage supplies all with arms.

Forgiveness is good for the body and soul. Medically, people who remain angry are susceptible to hypertension and related diseases. "Re-living unsuccessful or humiliating situations in the past hurt over and over again and prove bad for your health," says Dr Redfold Williams.

Simply remembering an incident that made a person angry has proved to be stressful for the heart. Negative feelings that cause stress have also been linked to high blood pressure and increased susceptibility to other illnesses. While terrible hurt may take only minutes to inflict, forgiving the perpetrator often requires more time. Initially, we experience negative feelings such as anger, sadness and shame. Then we try to make sense of what happened.

Ultimately, we learn to see the person who hurt us through new eyes. Some people never reach the final stages of forgiveness. Those hurt in childhood by people they loved and trusted may find the process particularly difficult. Yet, even partial forgiveness can be beneficial. Forgiveness can occur without anybody else's involvement or awareness.

The people who are forgiven may never realise they wronged us or never know we forgave them. What is important is that we let go of our anger. Hurtful experiences teach us not to be victimised again and to refrain from victimising others. Forgiveness leads to inner peace, once we have forgiven, we can laugh more, feel more deeply, become more connected to others.

And the good feeling we generate will lead to even greater healing. If we want to move towards a future of forgiving but do not know how to start, we may follow these suggestions given by Swami Paramananda in his Book of Daily Thoughts and Prayers that forgiving the slights by strangers readies us for the tougher task of forgiving major hurts. We can express our anger or disappointment with a trusted friend or counsellor.

This allows us the strengthening experience of being heard. We can let go of our feeling without the danger of saying or doing anything we will regret later. Anger-releasing methods such as punching a pillow can help. If we are not so much angry as sad, we may keep a journal. By all means we should avoid negative thinking and expression of anger such as driving dangerously, slamming doors or breaking things.

We can spell out the truth of what happened as we experienced it without blaming or judging. It is better to use the "I" statement: "I feel I do not understand" and so on. We may describe the impact of the person's behaviour on us and express our feelings to resolve the issue.

Creative Forgiveness
Springs from Love

By Janina Gomes

E need to find truth, love and forgiveness even in the midst of hatred, destruction and pride. Napoleon said: "What astonishes me most in this world is the inability of force to create anything. In the long run the sword is always beaten by the spirit." In so saying, Napoleon touched upon an important principle of forgiveness. That forgiveness is creative and it springs from love. It is the ability to embrace the pain of injury to oneself, while extending one's hands in love.

Forgiving is not easy. The hurt that others inflict on us haunts us from the past and sullies our future. Unfortunately, we tend to identify forgiving with only forgetting. But, by learning to live in the present, we will enable ourselves to embrace the pain of the infliction and heal ourselves as well as others.

Often, we let painful memories re-inflict pain. There's so much negativity attached to memory. To release memory, Raymond Studzinski says, is to see the injuring party as a human person who like oneself lives in an imperfect world fraught with stress and conflict. Forgiveness is to accept what has happened as past and not as the final word on the other or oneself.

That makes it creative. Edward Guinan says: "The heritage that martyrs, resisters and saints have left us is: 'Love can and must be lived today, despite the pain and difficulty of life. Tomorrow will carry the tenderness and peace which we live now'."

Most psychologists now acknowledge that an important aspect of forgiveness is to forgive oneself first for life exempts none from injury. To be good does not insulate one from hurt inflicted by others. Forgiveness meets the injurer with compassion. It acknowledges that we all have the same destructive tendencies and we carry within ourselves the ability to inflict pain on others.

We all feel the urge to seek justice for ourselves. Not all, however, are moved by compassion and mercy. Biblical images of God are of a forgiving God. God's mercy for erring humanity is portrayed as a mother's trembling womb. The image of a forgiving God is best epitomised by the figure of Jesus nailed to the cross who died with the words: "Father forgive them for they know not what they do." An unforgiving attitude and hate can lead to physical manifestations and psychosomatic illnesses. Dr Norman Vincent Peale reports the cure of a woman who suffered from a terrible itch on her arms. She resented her sister, who she felt had got a greater share of her father's estate on his death, because she was married and had children, whilst she was single.

Filled with hatred and pain, she developed physical symptoms. It was only when she was able to forgive and love her sister once again that she regained health and the ability to live life joyfully. Forgiveness is a grace from God. By ourselves, we are unable to forgive or forget. Grace from God creates and renews all life. Witness the courage and strength of spirit that enabled Gladys Staines to forgive the murderers of her husband and children.

Human beings are able to survive torture, death and ignominy because the human spirit is able to transcend it. Creative forgiveness enabled a Corrie Ten Boom to pardon her Nazi persecutor and spread the message of love; it inspired a Victor Frankl to enrich human psychology and psychiatry with his masterpiece, Man's Search for Meaning.

The spirit of love is the spirit of forgiveness which enables a defeated people to rise from the ashes to rebuild their lives. No hate in the world is as powerful as the forgiving power of love.

Take Responsibility For Your Actions

By Sadhu Vishwamurtidas

 NE of the most difficult and painful things to do in life is to admit one's mistakes.

When Neil Armstrong set foot on the moon, the first words he meant to say and which he had practised several times were: "That's a small step for a man, but a giant leap for mankind." What he actually uttered was a contradiction: "That's a small step for man but a giant leap for mankind."

But no one has acknowledged this error so far. Most of us hesitate to confess our mistakes. We are equally reluctant to express regret, and it is a rare person who tries to make amendments or even simply render a heartfelt apology. It is this reluctance of most people to admit that they've committed a mistake that forms the root of much human strife.

An unforgiving, unrepentant nature — whether among individuals, families, communities or nations — is responsible for misunderstandings that lead to enmity and hatred. Asked what she thought was most needed in the coming century, the celebrated historian Barbara Tuchman, a Pulitzer prize winner, said: "Personal responsibility... taking responsibility for your behaviour and not forever supposing that society must forgive you because it's not your fault". The mistake may not be totally one's own. But usually, in some subtle way — either through action, reaction or even inaction — we play our role poorly.

A teenager had just passed his driving test and was eager to drive his father's car. His father agreed. He asked his son to drop him at a place that was some 18 miles from home before he took the car for servicing. The father then wanted his son to pick him up at four in the afternoon so that they could go home together.

The boy dropped off his father, took the car to the garage and went to watch a film. Losing track of time, he continued to watch the film until 6 p.m. Afraid his father would scold him for being late and would never give him the car again, the boy collected the car, arrived at the appointed place and said, "Dad, I'm sorry I'm late but it took the mechanic longer than usual to service the car." "Son. I phoned the garage," his father replied. "The car was ready at 4 p.m." The boy looked down. "I'm sorry, but I went to watch a film." "Son, I'm very angry," replied the father after a moment of thought. "But not with you. I'm angry with myself. Where did I go wrong as a father? Why did you have to lie to me? Take the car home. I will introspect as I walk back."

The boy trailed behind his father, imploring him to sit inside the car. But his father continued walking silently, soul-searching all the way back home. Distraught, the son pledged to never again lie to his parents. In the story, not only the boy, his father, too, gets transformed. We all need to examine ourselves inside: have we gone wrong somewhere? For, it is almost impossible to change others, but we can change ourselves. If we all decided to do just that, there would be no need to change anybody else anyway.

The world would be transformed in a single stroke. Another thing that we need to change is our negative attitude to life. So few seem to be truly happy. Happiness is relative. It has little to do with money, fame or power. Why else do so many people who have all three, end up leading miserable lives? A positive attitude will make you grow. You will be able to achieve happiness and spread it around, making the world a better place to live in.

Forgive and Forget
To Create Amity

By Sudhamahi Regunathan

O forgive and to forget is not easy. A man who wished to be initiated into meditation went to a great sage and asked to be accepted as his disciple. The sage made him close his eyes gently and told him that the first step of meditation was to practise compassion. "Amity, compassion, amity, compassion," the sage repeated.

The man, however, was not concentrating. Finally, he opened his eyes and begged to be allowed to say something. "I can wish everybody well but my neighbour. I have a lawsuit against him. Can I leave him out?" The master laughed gently and said, "Leave out the whole world, just concentrate on your neighbour. Wish him well and you would have learnt the greatest secret of conquering aversions and attachments."

"Remember all that which supports your progress, brings you happiness and forget all that which impedes your progress, hinders positive thoughts," says Acharya Mahaprajna. "It is as important to learn to be forgetful as it is to learn to remember. If you remember the hurtful or the detrimental incidents, you are carrying an unnecessary burden with you and this will lead you to failure." To forgive and forget: they come as a pair, for unless you forget you cannot forgive and unless you forgive you cannot forget. This is what the eight-day Jaina festival of Paryushan and Kshama-yachana Divas or Samvatsari is all about.

Fasting is an important component; it is a symbol of restraint. On the last day, people visit each other and seek forgiveness for anything that they may have said or done to cause pain to others, knowingly or unknowingly.

Jain monks and nuns observe this sentiment throughout the year. Every evening, they perform what is known as the pratikraman where they get in touch with their inner self. They seek forgiveness for all the acts of violence that may have occurred in their interaction with the outside world. They seek this forgiveness not only from fellow humans but also from all living beings.

The festival is an opportunity to cleanse oneself. Just as a bath cleanses the body, and makes one feel lighter, this festival is meant to cleanse the soul, to make it lighter. One can relieve oneself of all tensions. When we eat or drink, we are quenching our hunger and thirst. We are satisfying one kind of need. Similarly, to seek forgiveness is the need of the spirit. It brings nutrition to the spirit and rejuvenates it.

Therefore, the spirit of this festival is important. If it is celebrated by just verbally seeking forgiveness, it is a routine, and can become a meaningless tradition; it gets reduced to being a ritual little understood. It should be more than that. Mahavira believed in equality to such an extent that he said if one forgives and the other is forgiven, it introduces inequality in society. So both sides should seek forgiveness and forgive. The meaning of forgiveness is limitless affection or amity. The most dominant cause of hatred is ahankar or arrogance. If we are able to overcome arrogance and develop humane qualities, we can access amity in no time. An essential prerequisite for spiritual fulfilment is being able to forgive.

The experience of divine forgiveness and pardon is universal, reaching to supplicants in all the world's religions. When anger is overcome, the spirit of forgiveness springs in the soul and the soul experiences infinite happiness.

Day of Forgiveness And Thanksgiving

By Andalib Akhter

ESTIVALS have a great value in human life. Occasional celebration of festivals breaks the monotony of our day-to-day life and brings cheer to all. For enjoyment and merrymaking, different religions have established specific time and dates. Islam, too, is not indifferent towards this joyful practice. Eid-ul-Fitr is one of the two annual festivals of Muslims, celebrated the world over.

Eid marks the end of Ramadan or fasting and is an act of collective thanksgiving to Allah for the reward of Ramadan and giving strength to believers to keep fasts and worship for a whole month. It is a day of forgetting old grudges and ill-feeling towards other fellow human beings.

It is the occasion for showing joy for the health, strength and opportunities Allah has bestowed on a believer to fulfil his obligations of fasting and performing good deeds during the holy month of Ramadan. Instead of commemorating an event from the past, Islam has prescribed Eid, the first day of Shawwal, the tenth month of the Islamic calendar as an annual festival for Muslims when they themselves undertake a great form of worship, the Roza.

This is expected to remind a person that he should not rely on the accomplishments of one's ancestors, but, undertake virtuous acts oneself to please the Almighty. Islam follows a unique approach in celebrating Eid. Unlike the festivals of other religions that usually comprise rejoicing through dancing, singing and playing, Islam has prescribed a simple yet graceful way to observe the festival.

It is mandatory for all well-off Muslims to start their day by paying Sadaqat-ul-Fitr, an obligatory charity to the poor of the society, so that they may enjoy the day along with others and may not be worried about earning their livelihood at least on the day of celebrations. Sadaqat-ul-Fitr is an obligation for every Muslim who owns 613.35 grams of silver or its equivalent, either in the form of money, ornaments, stock-in-trade, or goods beyond one's normal needs.

93

Every person who owns such an amount has to pay Sadaqat-ul-Fitr, not only on his behalf but on behalf of his minor children as well. The prescribed amount of Sadaqat-ul-Fitr is 1.75 kg of wheat or money of the same value. Every year the amount is fixed. This charity is given to the poor and needy, widows, disabled persons and orphans. It cannot be adjusted in the wages of the servant, or be given for the construction of a mosque. It is advised that the Sadaqat-ul-Fitr is paid before performing the 'Eid prayer', but it can be paid before the 'Eid day'.

However, if a person has failed to pay on time, he should pay it as soon as possible. After paying the obligatory charity, Muslims proceed to mosques or Eid Gaah to offer the Eid prayers collectively. Here they present themselves before Allah, the Creator, and offer a special namaz or prayer, to receive the blessings of the Almighty.

During prayer, people from different strata of society stand shoulder-to-shoulder and bow and prostrate before Allah. All distinction of class and status disappear. After the prayer, they embrace one another and say, "Eid Mubarak" to one another.

Since Eid-ul-Fitr is the day on which Muslims break their month-long fast, it is preferable to eat before going for the prayer. Prophet Muhammad had the habit of eating an odd number of dates before going for Eid prayer. While going to the special namaz, Muslims generally do takbeer, or the glorification of Almighty as prescribed in the Qur'an, which says, "You should complete the prescribed period and then you should glorify Allah for having guided you so that you may be grateful to Him."

The believer is expected to follow a particular guidance before performing the special prayers. At the beginning of the day of Eid-ul-Fitr, one should wake up early in the morning and after taking a bath, he should put on new or best available clothes. After the namaz, Muslims are supposed to celebrate the day in a responsible manner greeting one another at home and in the neighbourhood. People visit each other's homes and partake of festive meals with special dishes, beverages and desserts.

Children receive gifts and sweets on this special occasion. Islam advises not to violate the limits prescribed and never to indulge in acts that are prohibited, especially on this auspicious day.

Lent: Time to Fast, Forgive and Give

By Janina Gomes

ENT is the 40-day period of preparation before Easter. For Christians worldwide, it is a time for repentance, fasting and almsgiving, all of which call for a change of mind and heart. Gerard Hughes says a change of mind and heart cannot in a sense be achieved by us alone, as all Christian renewal starts not from self-effort but by attentiveness to God, who alone is good.

It is God who does the transforming. A real change of mind and heart means an inner surrendering of our mind and heart to God, so that whatever we do, we do in his Spirit. Hughes calls this transformation a lifelong process and says the nearer we approach to this surrender, the more conscious we become of layer upon layer of resistance in our spirit.

It is only those who are near to God who know what sin is. Our mind seems to be constructed in layers. There are top layers, which do not affect our deeper consciousness, where there is not only an assimilation of factual knowledge but also of emotional experience. It is in these deep layers of consciousness that real change occurs and the longest and most difficult journey is the journey from the top layer of our minds to the heart, where God is waiting to welcome us. Repentance means effecting change at these deeper layers of consciousness.

Christians are urged to pray, fast and give alms during Lent. Sincere prayer is at the heart of all renewal. This prayer is directed at bringing us closer to God, so that we realise our sinfulness and our utter dependence on the Supreme Being. However, our prayer will be effective only if it enables us to recognise the creative action of God's Spirit in our lives and enables us to reach out to others.

That is why prayer has to be accompanied by fasting and almsgiving. Many people fast for health reasons or for other reasons not inspired by spiritual motives. Others believe that by fasting they can, through a barter arrangement with God, through some ritualistic magic, win acceptance for themselves. That is why the prophet of the Old Testament Jeremiah wrote, "The heart is more devious than any other thing, perverse too: who can pierce its secrets?"

Fasting is valuable not only when it has a salutary effect upon us, but also when it helps us to feel more compassion for the millions who 'fast' daily, and prompts us to contribute towards alleviating the problem of poverty. But fasting alone does not necessarily bring us closer to God.

Isaiah, in the Old Testament, said, "Fasting like yours today will never make your voice heard on high. Is not this the sort of fast that pleases me: it is the Lord Yahweh who speaks to break unjust fetters, to let the oppressed go free, and break every yoke, to share your bread with the hungry and shelter the homeless poor, to clothe the man you see to be naked and not turn from your kin".

Fasting from wrongdoing is more important than fasting from food. Hughes also speaks of an inner fasting of the mind, fasting from walking along those dark inner paths of self-pity, of blaming others, of relishing the failures of others, of nursing grievances. Lent is also the time to give alms. Rather than give condescendingly, charity has to come from the heart, to remind us that we should feel empathy rather than pity for the unfortunate.

Almsgiving not only includes works of mercy such as caring for the sick and the homeless, it includes a much more difficult task, which is to forgive. Lent is a time to ask God for forgiveness; it is also a time for us to forgive one another, a time to let go past resentments, breaking down the barriers which divide us.

Jesus is said to have spent 40 days in the desert where he was subject to various temptations. These consisted of Jesus being expected to turn loaves into bread since he was hungry, to throw himself down from the parapet because he was divine and the angels would not allow him to be hurt, and the promise that he would be given all the splendours of the world if he fell down and worshipped the devil.

In the temptations, Jesus uncovered the deceits of the evil one and said, "You must worship the Lord your God, and serve Him alone." Lent is the time to surrender ourselves wholly to God and to concentrate only on the Supreme Being, so that our lives may be transformed.

Inverting the Pyramid: Leaders as Servants

By Chirdeep S Bagga

EADERSHIP is often associated with power. Today, the term has acquired negative connotations, particularly in politics. One has come to question the relative importance of being recognised as a "leader". What we sorely need are individuals who both lead by their service and example and follow the universally accepted principles of responsible living.

We are beginning to see that traditional autocratic and hierarchical models of leadership are slowly yielding to a newer model. This model — of leaders as servants — will simultaneously enhance the personal growth of the led and improve the quality of our many institutions through a combination of individual and community teamwork in decision-making infused with ethical and caring behaviour.

Servant-leadership is a practical philosophy concerned with the ethical use of power and authority. Servant-leaders believe that power and authority are for helping others grow, not for ruling, exploiting, or gaining advantage by setting individuals or groups against one another.

Robert Greenleaf, the "grandfather of the modern empowerment movement in business leadership" who coined the term, described servant-leadership as follows: "The servant-leader is servant first... It begins with a natural feeling that one wants to serve first. Then conscious choice brings one to aspire to lead... The best test, and the most difficult to administer, is: Do those served grow as persons? Do they, while being served, become healthier, wiser, freer, more autonomous, more likely themselves to become servants?"

Servant-leadership challenges the notion of the traditional leader as a stand-alone hero. This model advocates a group-oriented approach to analysis and decision-making as a means of strengthening institutions, and of improving society. It also emphasises the power of persuasion and consensus over the old "top-down" form of leadership. Some liken this to turning the hierarchical pyramid upside down, so that in the mind of the servant-leader, the needs of his employees, customers, constituents and community become the most important reason for a company's existence. To a considerable extent, the servant-leadership approach is one which is best exemplified by the Japanese model of management and leadership.

Followers of Greenleaf's philosophy have identified 10 characteristics of a servant-leader: listening, empathy, healing, awareness, persuasion, conceptualisation, foresight, stewardship, commitment to the growth of people, and building community. Some of these come more naturally to some people than others. By their nature, characteristics such as empathy, healing, and stewardship are more difficult to learn and develop than the others.

But these are necessary for successful servant-leadership. Listening, awareness, persuasion, conceptualisation, foresight, growth, and building community are all learnable skills and servant-leaders can continually develop these.

John Wright, the Indian cricket team coach, has the attributes of a servant-leader. He has worked to build a strongly interdependent team — one in which players listen to each other and introspect to find the resources to make a difference. In a team that glorified individualism, Wright's ability to convince superstars to put aside their egos for the common good contributed to the team's success.

India's new prime minister, Manmohan Singh, looks to be enshrined in the philosophy of servant-leadership. But only time will tell if the Indian polity is mature enough to appreciate the virtues of leadership inspired by humility.

There's More to Life Than Striking Deals

By Sadhguru Jaggi Vasudev

F you really want the best deal in life, stop making deals. Yet, your very demeanour should be such that your client is simply bowled over. This is not a trick. The deal will happen if it's necessary; it won't happen if it's not. It is for the well-being of both parties, so it must be needed by both of you.

Once we're in this world, there are transactions, personal or otherwise. Let's say you're in love. If you are not fully involved, you will try to strike a deal. Once a bachelor who had been wooing an attractive woman for long, mustered the courage to propose to her. "There are quite a lot of advantages to being a bachelor," he began, " but there comes a time when one longs for the companionship of another being."

"A being who will regard one as perfect, as an idol to be worshipped and treated as one's absolute own, who will be kind and faithful when times are tough and hard, who will share one's joys and sorrows." To his delight he saw a sympathetic gleam in her eyes. She nodded and then said, " I think it's a great idea! Can I help you choose a pup?"

So to get mileage out of a deal, you have to first assess the level of intelligence of the other party. If you just give of yourself and see how both of you can be benefited from the deal, whenever it is possible, it will happen. Of course, deals are subject to many other conditions such as market situations, economic conditions or the world situation, but if you establish your inner way of being and are doing the best you can do, then what has to happen, according to your capability, will happen.

What you can't do, won't happen anyway. Even if you break your head it won't happen, but that's okay. However, if your whole life is about making deals, you will be miserable. The devil is always making a deal with somebody. God never made a deal with anybody. Maybe, you haven't attained to your full Divine nature, but at least in this case let us imitate God for a while.

God doesn't make deals. Deals will be offered to you in so many ways. In a way, everybody is just a businessman. Everybody is trying to pull off some deal: some in the market place, another maybe at home, in the temple, and others even with their spiritual process, but everybody is trying to pull off some kind of a deal. When you get a good deal, you are civilised and nice but if a deal goes bad, you yell and scream.

You need not be superhuman, capable of doing everything. If you don't do what you're capable of doing, that's when it's not okay; that's when you have failed. So don't worry about always pulling off deals, deals and more deals. Just learn to offer yourself, which is the best possible thing that you can offer to the whole situation. Then, naturally, people will take it if it's what they need.

Whether you talk to a taxi driver for a minute, or you talk to your boss, or speak to your client, husband, wife or child, every transaction is affecting your life. Now the problem with you is that you hold one transaction above the other. You involve yourself more with one and less with the other. It won't work like that. All these things are needed for you to have a fruitful life. Why don't you just fall in love with the whole situation? Then, work becomes effortless.

Mantra of Volunteering: Giving is Receiving

By Anant Nadkarni

OR those in the corporate sector who believe that their skills, talents, expertise, knowledge and wisdom constitute an immense 'wealth' that should be distributed among the underprivileged in society, volunteering for shrama and gyanadaan comes as a great opportunity.

'Charity' or 'philanthropy' works through the channels of charity trusts and societies to give a part of the money-wealth earned by the 'better-off' to compensate the 'worse-off'. Volunteering, too, is a similar "institution". People find new ways to reach out to those in need and serve them, through this "institution". Corporate bodies have come to realise that instilling the right attitudes in their volunteers is the most efficient way to fulfil their corporate social responsibility.

Volunteering, unlike charity, addresses the issues of dependence and independence much more proactively and directly. It fosters self-reliance and addresses the issues of dignity and empowerment to create a culture of self-help. Charity continues to address events like calamities and disasters and other images of despair — where pure funding is still a dire need. But volunteering is a developmental effort to bring about social change, to build capacity in people to work together. It aims to create a sense of responsibility so that people can take charge of their future.

To bring out the best in volunteering as an 'institution of development' is to recognise the spirit of service as its basic guiding principle. Volunteering can take more specific forms of mentoring, problem-solving, fund-raising, and teaching and training. It can also take up bigger challenges or can just be a way of having fun. But volunteering is not for attention seekers. It is not for those who have an insatiable desire to be in the limelight. It is to preclude this possibility that one must start with the spirit of service.

In a feedback from a wide cross-section of corporate employees, a 27-year-old HR professional recommends that the basic intent in all volunteering work should be self-development: said in the words of Swami Vivekananda "Atmano Mokshartam, Jagata Hitayacha" (only for one's own liberation should one serve society).

This brings us to a new paradigm in development — where growth is not only about the 'other' in society, but it is about a holistic process involving everyone concerned.

Development is then about identifying 'mindsets' and is about a fundamental change through reflection, transformation and breakthroughs in one's own perception. The locus of control for change is brought within.

As Neale Walsch says, "It is easier to change what you are doing than to see how to change another." Another prerequisite for planned change or development is to create a quality of leadership in which there is increased trust within a community. This is a kind of "social-process-work" facilitated by volunteers. In such a case, the facilitator's own disposition to life becomes critical.

The facilitator has to be a more complete personality and be a fairly evolved and a mature being. Because, this process involves taking the 'community' or group of people into a whole new 'way-of-being'. And, the facilitator has to lead this process of complete change. As Albert Einstein said, "A problem cannot be solved by being in the same condition in which it was created." A facilitator then should demonstrate personal abilities for bringing about a radical change, and cannot be part of the problem, stuck in one's own 'story' or obsessed by some 'ism'.

Volunteering is to be regarded as a spiritual journey. As one business development manager in an IT company, who brought computer education to a municipal corporation, recently said, "I am drawn into this work as if unknowingly by divine design." Another qualified social worker, and deputy manager-HR, admitted, "I feel more relaxed now and believe in the confidence that we have achieved much more as a team."

A PR manager and community champion says, "It has broadened my vision and I experience something more authentic happening to my life." These are just a few recent responses to reiterate that volunteering can impact the community when those serving and sharing talent have their intent and motive deeply rooted in self-actualisation. Ultimately, as Edmund Hillary said, "It is not the mountain we conquer, but ourselves."

Love is the Driving Force of Life

By Janina Gomes

RUE love does not lie in receiving but in giving. Love is the driving force and is the heart of all religions. Love is the energy which comes from the willingness to cooperate with God's plan of creation, says psychiatrist T B D'Netto. In his work titled Reaching out in Love, D'Netto says that love is the force that motivates all people of goodwill, as it did Mother Teresa of Calcutta.

Christian revelation emphasises that the most important aspect of God's nature is love. God's love is a compassionate love. Jesus preached this basic message and invited all his followers to be like him: "This is my commandment that you love one another as I have loved you."

D'Netto sees the life of Jesus on earth as a life motivated by compassionate love. In asking his followers to love one another in this way, Jesus invited them to be compassionate like him and to forgive one another. Loving God, according to the Bible, is not an option but a commandment. He spells out the practical implications of this commandment.

Loving God implies loving his creation and especially human beings. Analysing the saying of Jesus: "You shall love your neighbour as yourself," D'Netto says that since love is an activity and an attitude involving knowledge of the object of love, respect, care and concern for the object, self-love or loving oneself is acceptable especially since it is a commandment to love one's neighbour in the same manner.

In many schools of thought, self-love and love for others are considered mutually exclusive and even incompatible. Calvin spoke of self-love as a 'pest' because it signified selfishness. For Freud self-love was the same as narcissism and, hence, an immature love. To overcome this difficulty, Paul Tillich, a Christian theologian, suggested the term 'self-love' be replaced by 'self-affirmation' or 'self-acceptance'.

While emphasising the importance of true, genuine human love, D'Netto believes that love is often like water, open to contamination. The contamination can come through intention due to jealousy, rivalry or pride and prejudice. It could come about unintentionally due to ignorance, misunderstanding or simply the weakness and frailty of human nature.

Sometimes, what may be mistaken for true love both by the lover and loved one, is really the expression of a will to pleasure or the will to power. Other contaminants of love may be emotional needs caused by loneliness, self-preservation, fear or ego problems like pathological self-love.

Suggesting that the art of sharing is at the root of all love, D'Netto says that since human beings are part of God's creation, a natural consequence of loving God is loving people. All religions teach the concept of universal love or universal charity.

An important offshoot of love is altruism based on love and respect for the other person. Altruism which is connected with human emotional development leads to expenditure of time, energy, money and possessions. Describing the different nuances of love found in the Sanskrit and Greek languages like bhakti or reverential love for God in Sanskrit, maitri or sneha to describe love in friendship between companions called phiha in Greek, karuna for compassionate love, madhurya for a beloved's love, D'Netto says what often leads to confusion in the English language is that the word 'love' is used to convey many meanings.

Often it is ignorance of these finer differences that leads to confusion and misunderstanding. True love which is at the root of all creation must result in a 'reaching out to others' spirit. Even with the tremendous advances in technology and research available in modern times, something still seems to be missing. For him, this missing dimension is the spiritual dimension. This spiritual dimension is characterised by compassionate love.

If love inspires both individuals and the world, it will lead to the opening of a new dimension altogether in human existence. That is why D'Netto advocates the practice of loving others and reaching out to them in love.

Perfect the Art of Giving Graciously

By Seema Burman

UMAN beings are made up of a sensory system — therefore, we indulge in sensory pleasures; that's our destiny, say some. However true this might be, we must attempt to rise above them if we are to discover the Divine hidden within.

Aware of the difficulties in controlling the senses, ancient philosophers evolved practical methods of daan or almsgiving, vrat or fast, tapas or austerities and dhyan or meditation. Daanam means the will to share one's wealth with others. But why should we give away anything?

Giving helps to purify the Self. Sharing wealth requires purification of mind, atmashuddhi, and control of senses, damashca. Give, but without pitying the needy. Pity only inflates the ego whereas humility deflates it. Ramakrishna cringed at the very idea of feeling pity towards another fellow human being, who is, after all, an image of Consciousness.

On Vivekananda's advice, millionaire Rockefeller reluctantly handed over his first cheque for a public cause. He expected the young swami to be thankful to him — but Vivekananda replied: "It is for you to thank me." He said that it is the receiver who obliges the giver by accepting and not the other way round; since men are images of the Super Consciousness one must be able to see in the receiver an image of God.

Krishna explains to Arjuna that as long as one identifies oneself with the body, all activities — be it eating, reading, thinking, worshipping or almsgiving — are covered under the three gunas or characteristics: Saatvik, rajasik and tamasik. When you give whole-heartedly to the deserving, without expecting returns, it is saatvik. For, when one expects some service in return, it is a transaction, not charity. Give to a worthy person, says Krishna, at the right time and place.

Humility is the mark of a genuinely generous person. Sufi poet Rahim, known for his generosity, gave with downcast eyes. He said it was God who was giving through him. Rajasik charity is when something is given with a view to receiving in return (wedding gifts), or when one expects good fruit of the action (I will get promotion by donating to the poor; I will get IT relief; my name will appear in the paper) or when donation is given reluctantly (I must give to please the organiser).

Tamasik charity is when the gift is given at the wrong place or time to unworthy persons, without respect or with disdain (bribes to get work done; money thrown at the poor, wounding their self-respect).

Referring to a passage in the Taittiriya Upanishad, Sri Ranganathananda says: "Shraddhaya deyam", give with faith, "Ashraddhaya adeyam", do not give without faith, "Shriya deyam", give with a sense of plenty, "Bhiya deyam", give with a feeling of fear for the cause is great and the amount is so small, "Hriya deyam", give with humility, "Samvida deyam", give with the knowledge of the purpose to which you are giving.

Daan is a practical process that gradually helps in eliminating one's attachment to maya or illusion. But, say the saints, it can be possible only when God is uppermost in your thoughts. As Ramakrishna Paramhansa said to his devotees, "Beware of kamini, lust, and kanchan, gold, as these are the two great temptations that disturb the mind and sway man from the path of love for God."

When you think of God, be free of all attachments, think only of the Super Consciousness. At the time of death, one has to leave one's entire wealth but those who cling to it throughout their lives, worry about their material possessions even while dying. "While leaving the mortal body, one whose mind dwells in Me, comes to me, have no doubt," assures Krishna.

Unconditional Love Brings Joy to All

By Swami Chaitanya Keerthi

LL of us need to believe that we are loved and are lovable. We begin life secure in our mother' s love, swaddled in our innocence. Love was never in question, but over time, we become increasingly unsure...

In The Path to Love, Deepak Chopra says that by bringing spirituality back into our relationships, we can discover a world of depth and meaning. He says: "You were created to be completely loved and to be completely lovable for your whole life."

The problems begin when we start taking love for granted and get possessive about life. We deny freedom and space to the people we love — our children, spouse, friend.

Unknowingly, we start killing our love. And we create bondage for ourselves, too, when we curb the freedom of the person we love.

Osho says: "Freedom is a higher value than love." Love stifles and gets stifled when it encroaches upon the space of another. Love blossoms in the space of freedom, in breeziness. Once we realise the nature of true love, we no longer 'fall' in love — we actually 'rise' in love. At this point love becomes unconditional. We give our love and feel grateful to all those who receive it, because this way we unburden ourselves.

Osho says when the clouds are full of rain water, they have to shower. It is their need. Similarly, when we become full of love, it is our need to give our love to one and all. Then we are not concerned whether or not we receive love in return. We simply enjoy giving. Conditional love is attachment; it is bondage, so it is also an illusion. We say we want to be free but are we brave enough to be alone? We fear loneliness. We fear being unoccupied.

We started out looking for love, but maybe we were really looking for attachment. Our need may have been attachment all along. Love was the way to attain it, the bait.

Unconditional love will not become attachment. But the moment you say to your partner, "Love only me", you begin to possess her. And in possessing, you're making your lover into an object to be used. Immanuel Kant said that to treat another person as a means is an immoral act.

In other words, if you see your lover as being there for your gratification, or to fulfil your sexual desires, or to provide something else for you... you're reducing your partner to an object. You are in bondage — so inevitably, you'll eventually desire freedom. You will be bored by what you have and yearn for what you don't have. Or you could try to be free even while 'possessing' your partner, causing a struggle.

Osho says, "I want to be a free person, and yet I want you to be possessed by me; you want to retain your freedom and still possess me — this is the struggle... We must remain individuals and we must move as independent, free consciousness. We can come together, we can merge into each other, but no one possesses. Then there is no bondage and then there is no attachment." Love becomes a blessing, a real celebration when love breathes fresh air free from possessiveness and jealousy. There should be no judgement, no blame, no expectations and no attempts to control. The soul can grow only in freedom — and unconditional love provides freedom.

Osho says: "My message is beyond biology and theology... Love is nothing but sharing of your consciousness with as many people as possible; not only with people, but with animals, trees, birds, clouds, stars."

Discover the Truth, Set Yourself Free

By Trishla Jain

RISHNA'S teaching was meant to facilitate the merging of Arjun's individualised consciousness with the infinite consciousness. Krishna recommended 'karma-yoga' and 'bhakti-yoga' as two methods of reaching the divine. Arjun asks, "Renunciation of action and discipline — which is better?"

Krishna replies: "Both effect good beyond measure; but of the two, discipline in action surpasses renunciation of action." Krishna advocates that the only way to attain everlasting equanimity is to free the mind of bondage to the 'worldly' world and understand the nature of the self to become one with the eternal spirit.

Krishna asserts action cannot be avoided, and should be performed without consideration of the "fruit of action". Progression on the ladder of karma was associated with good action: one who did good things in life moved up the ladder.

However, as related by Krishna in the Gita, good action is by no means enough. Good action merely implies the appearance of doing good to achieve good. True enlightenment, the very top of the ladder, may only be achieved by controlling the senses, sublimating the body and even the self to merge with the eternal consciousness.

The Gita elevates the requirements for attaining Nirvana from mere progression on the ladder by performing good to actually becoming pure from within. The divine seeker must first condition his mind and heart to be separate from his actions and those around him. "A man of eternal renunciation is one who neither hates nor desires; beyond dualities, he is easily freed from bondage."

Krishna tells Arjun that he must free himself from transient, undulating negative-positive pulls of the world. In this effort,

Arjun must have, "Detachment, uninvolvement with sons, wife and home, constant equanimity in fulfilment and frustration". He must perform all his duties to his family, without the hope of reward.

By mastering the senses, one can overcome the separation between the worldly body and being. "Seeing, hearing, touching, smelling, eating, walking, sleeping, breathing, the disciplined man who knows reality should think, 'I do nothing at all. It is the senses that engage in sense objects'." Krishna says that this can be done by meditation focused on breath or by understanding that the body, through its senses, engages in action.

The self begins to transform itself into its virgin state. The enlightenment-seeker is just physically in the prison of the 'worldly' world but mentally, emotionally, spiritually separate from it. Death and doom must be seen as being equal to birth, celebration and creation as dualities of the universe.

After understanding the nature of the self, the knowledge-seeker becomes one with the Brahmn. The Brahmn, or the infinite spirit, is described as "imperishable, ineffable, unmanifest, omnipresent, inconceivable, immutable at the summit of existence". It is a state of pure consciousness, when a person's very being completely comprehends the nature of its internal state and the external universe. Moving up on the ladder of karma to break the cycle of birth and death is an internal adventure, not something that can be done merely by good action, meditation and renunciation of the material world.

Krishna teaches that it is not necessary to actually leave the confines of the birth-death cycle to be absolutely free from it. By controlling the senses and mind, and subsequently performing worldly action as sacrifice, we will know the truth that will set us free.

Your Destiny is What You Make of It

By Sadhguru Jaggi Vasudev

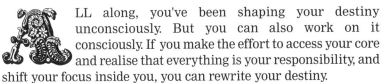LL along, you've been shaping your destiny unconsciously. But you can also work on it consciously. If you make the effort to access your core and realise that everything is your responsibility, and shift your focus inside you, you can rewrite your destiny.

All the time, your focus is scattered, because what you consider is 'you' and 'yours' is your house, car, wife, child, pet, education, position and power. If you are stripped of all these things, you will feel like a nobody. So what you call yourself is what is spread around you. 'You' means it is you, not this carpet, wall, child, or anything else. 'You' is just you. Right now, you're not an established being; you are a scattered being. You are not you; you are a crowd. The crowd's fate is always predestined. Once you act as an individual, the indivisible self can no longer be divided; it is this. It cannot be here and there. Once you become a true individual, your destiny is within your grasp; it is yours.

Those who are in a hurry to grow spiritually avoid getting into marriage, children and relationships because the moment you have a spouse, you get identified with 'this one'. Once you have children, you get identified with them. Now, 'you' includes them also. Once you get identified with them, one by one, you get identified with too many things. Your identity gets scattered.

However, searching for the real 'you' does not mean denial of family or social situations. The root of all identification is in the two fundamental accumulations: body and mind. Once removed from these two, 'you' become free from all identifications. In this freedom, you become the master of your own destiny.

The body is the source of all attachments. But you don't have to keep searching for non-attachment somewhere else. You don't have to go about distancing this and that in your life, but once you get scattered, your destiny becomes preordained. Whichever way your karma is, it just goes that way.

The significance of Sanyasa or Brahmacharya is just this: shifting the whole focus to you. When I say you, it is just 'you', not your body or mind. If you are unable to be like that, you just choose one more identity. When you say 'you', make it 'you and your Guru'. You attach yourself to the Guru without any hesitation, because you have no entanglements from the other side. You can get as entangled as you want with him; for he is not going to get entangled.

The moment you are ripe, you can drop the relationship. With other relationships, it is never so. If you get entangled, even if you want to become free, the other will not let you go. Either you can reshape your destiny or, if such awareness does not come, the Guru can help you do it. You just create a longing to grow, to dissolve, to know. What has to happen will happen. Once you become an individual, your destiny becomes yours. If your destiny is in your hands, you would naturally choose freedom and not bondage because the deepest longing of every life is to become free from the very process that one refers to as life or death.

So once your destiny is happening in awareness, the next step will just happen by itself, because life within you has the intelligence to choose freedom, not bondage. Only because your destiny is being created in unawareness, you go about weaving bondage around yourself.

Your Life is a See-saw, Make the Most of It

By Ullhas Pagey

E have our ups and downs, successes and failures, elations and disappointments. Nothing is certain but change. Winners turn losers and vice versa, for that is the law of nature. Impermanence is a permanent feature of life. The best way to deal with the transiency is to learn to maximise our spiritual quotient.

Stephen Covey in his Seven Habits of Highly Effective People elaborates on habits we need to acquire in order to be effective. Twenty virtues have been elaborated by Krishna in the Bhagavad Gita. These virtues, if perfected, can lead us to the Ultimate Truth.

The first virtue is humility, amanitvam. Having acquired wealth or education, position or power, some turn arrogant. And this is the beginning of the end. That's why humility is considered the most important quality for spiritual evolvement.

The second quality refers to modesty, adambhitvam, the state of egolessness. It is the ego that generates most of the problems in our lives, whether at work or home. Humility and modesty go hand in hand. Achieving modesty also helps one in enhancing one's emotional quotient.

The third quality refers to non-violence, ahimsa, a concept promoted by spiritual leaders like Gautama Buddha and Mahatma Gandhi. Ahimsa not only refers to the physical injury but also to the psychological injury caused because of hurting somebody's feelings.

At the grosser level, it also implies use of decent language and resorting to polite behaviour. Forgiveness is the fourth quality. There is no virtue greater than the ability to forgive. Forthrightness, arjavam, the fifth desirable virtue, refers to transparency; to being straightforward. Our dealings with people should be straight, free of any hidden agenda.

Respect for the guru, purity of thought and action, consistency of purpose and self-restraint are other important qualities we should cultivate to face dualities in life.

Krishna also talks of detachment to the sense objects through vairagya. This quality assumes great significance in today's context when people are increasingly becoming more pleasure-seeking and materialistic.

Further, we should strive to eschew egotism. The basic thought of "My"ness is an antithesis to the spiritual seeker as it denotes attachment and no seeker can undertake the spiritual journey until and unless such thoughts are given up.

Birth, death, old age and sickness should be perceived as natural phenomena of life. Take them in your stride. During all these phases one should not become impatient with pain.

Swami Chinmayananda observes: "Unless the seeker is constantly conscious of the evil of pain in his present stage, he will not discover the necessary spiritual urge to seek the Divine Fields of Perfection. Such an attitude towards life would facilitate to reach the Ultimate Goal." Next, develop an attitude of non-attachment and avoid excessive affection and reliance on those who are near and dear. It does not, however, mean that we should not be very close but we should not be over-attached to them.

Above all, an unflinching devotion to the Divine, staying away from crowded places and company, love for solitude and lonely places, continuous indulgence in the knowledge of 'Self', and an everlasting focus on the 'Ultimate Knowledge' all add to complete the 20 virtues necessary to achieve spiritual uplift. Make these 20 virtues a habit and discover a whole new world of everlasting bliss. These 20 components of knowledge together constitute the 'True Knowledge'.

Interval Between Birth and Death

By K S Narayanaswamy

HO can measure the infinity of time? The flow of time is permanent; so it would flow on even if all the clocks in the world stopped ticking. Night and day, months and years roll on, but to the individual, the period of time between his birth and death assumes prime importance. From this measure of time emerges the ethical value of that time.

Depending on the waves of human aspirations from time to time, the ethical values of an era get shaped. The values of a period leave an impression on the life of any person who may live in that period. It directs the values of personal life and, according to his own inner wisdom, a person shapes his relationships with family and society.

Through day-to-day experience and inquisitiveness a person observes and stores in memory the actions and reactions around him, sculpting his own life, changing circumstances and making history.

At times he stands aloof, away from the flow of time, observing with wonder. He experiences in his inner consciousness that some insurmountable, vast, permanent power that is beyond speculation and description is working behind worldly happenings. The world does not run according to a single individual's imagination.

Worldly affairs go on forever, pushing the course of time to flow unexpectedly in different directions through a secret force operating as a sum total of all the great efforts.

The way a man resonates to the values of an era is predicated on which cultural tradition he is born into and also on the kind of environment he is brought up in. During his lifetime, prominent historical events and waves of thought continuously influence a thinking man, creating complex situations which can make him disillusioned at one time and rebellious at another.

Times change, taking people to unexpected destinations, creating challenges which often disappear by themselves. These events remind man of the limitations of human endeavour. Incapable of imagining the vast nature of innumerable possibilities at once, the human mind with its limited capabilities wanders in search of a supreme power for shelter.

After observing the complexity of life, a wise soul wrote in the Upanishad: "eshawasyamidam sarvam" — everything is pervaded by God. When a man reaches the fag end of his journey, many questions crowd his mind: How does one remain unattached in this complex karmic web of life? How does the last moment happen? What is beyond that? After much soul-searching, man finally surrenders to the thought that some invisible force has concealed the truth behind the facade of life.

Realising that the revelation of this truth is impossible through human efforts, man prays: "Oh Lord, the maker of the world, unravel the truth and its working principles." Akin to the mythological churning of the ocean, there is a parallel agitation going on in every mind — and what comes up could be nectar or poison or both. It is up to the individual to learn to discriminate between the two.

Life has to go forward in its entirety. How much did we acquire from whom? We keep acquiring right from birth. The sum total of acquired things even at the time of our birth is beyond imagination. When we ask the question — what did the world of my time get from me? — we might feel that one individual's contribution is no more than the equivalent of a small pebble on a huge beach.

The fact is that the common man — unobserved by anyone, incapable of making any impact, with no extraordinary quality — is still the central point of his time-era and this remains an undisputable truth.

The Golden Mean and Pairs of Opposites

By Akhil Chandra

E live in a world of opposites where gain and loss, good and bad, pleasure and pain, life and death are as inevitable as the two sides of a coin. Yet, there is an underlying unity between the two contrasts.

One of the principal polarities in life is the one between the male and female aspects of human nature. The sublime union between these two aspects is symbolised by Lord Shiva's depiction as a dynamic unification of the two, as the half-male, half-female Ardhanareeshwar. In real life, too, there is a constant dynamic interplay between the two extremes of opposites and one has to strike a balance between the two.

For this, we need to maintain a balance between good and bad, between winning and losing, and so on. This will help us to follow the path of right conduct in an unattached and fearless manner. In science, existence of opposite extremes in nature is best described by the concept of positively and negatively charged particles of matter which combine during chemical reaction to achieve neutrality.

Mathematically, also, equal positive and negative values add up to zero, mingling into oneness. The simple rhythmic motion of a pendulum has two opposite extremes of movement. The same principle is widely visible in the nature of day and night, light and darkness, heat and cold. According to Indian thought also opposites are merely two sides of the same reality and can ultimately be reconciled in a single whole.

The Bhagavad Gita asks us to lead the unattached life of a self-controlled man, a karma yogi, unmoved by pairs of opposites: "The Supreme Spirit is rooted in the knowledge of the self-controlled man whose mind is perfectly serene in the midst of pairs of opposites, such as cold and heat, joy and sorrow and honour and ignominy."

Chinese sages called this dynamic interplay of two extremes as Ying and Yang — positive and negative — and have extended this thought extensively to the function of daily life. The Sufi saw merging of opposites in the unity of Brahman, the world-soul, and Atman, the individual soul. The path to enlightenment, then, involves the realisation of this and moving beyond it, to where one sees everything as part of the ultimate reality.

Sufism says that it is not very important to distinguish between two opposites. It is more important to recognise the One that is hidden, and opposites are simply the manifestation of a basic oneness. Sufis believed that the 'real' world (maya) is made up of opposites and is illusory (mithya).

The philosophy of unification of opposites is omnipresent in Indian thought. The word 'yoga' comes from the Sanskrit word Yuj meaning to join or unite. It is the union of all aspects of the individual body, mind and soul. Hence, yoga reunites all opposites — mind and body, stillness and movement, masculine and feminine — in order to bring about reconciliation between them.

For everything, there is a complementary part representing the other part of extreme. In our daily life, we should reconcile the play of opposites. This will allow us the possibility of accommodating widely divergent human experiences in an underlying harmony, bringing newer prospects and ethical views for the exploration and mitigation of human suffering.

If we adopt the complementary approach to problems, we may discover to our pleasant surprise that seemingly irreconcilable points of view need not be contradictory but can make possible the striking of a balance between extremes. You cannot always win or lose or be happy or sad — so go on, find the Golden Mean.

Suffering Is In the State Of Our Mind

By Suresh Jindal

UDDHA observed that all of us experience three kinds of suffering. There is the 'suffering of suffering' — of illness, handicaps and wounds of the body. There is the 'suffering of the change in our conditions' — of happiness to sorrow, of fortune to misfortune, from euphoria to despair, from the blissful psychedelics of everlasting and eternal love to the bitterness of recrimination and blame. Finally, there is the suffering that is inherent and inevitable in just being born in the cycle of samsara.

A Buddhist is taught that all of creation is an interdependent web and that every sentient being desires happiness and freedom from suffering. Buddhists do not believe that everyone is inherently evil.

Harmful action is a result of wrong views and negative motions arising out of an illusion that phenomena and persons have permanent existence. The belief in permanence of our name, fame, wealth, health and beauty gives rise to self-grasping and self-cherishing attitudes, which disconnect us from the web of life.

We latch on to an 'I' and a 'me', which on investigation is found not to reside in the body, the mind, or in some undiscovered corner of the vast cosmos. Gratification of the body and mind is as impermanent as 'a bubble, a mirage, a dream or image of the moon reflected on a still lake'. The body, like all else, will disintegrate and dissolve.

In the conventional world, all phenomena and selves exist by nomination, labels and convention. The criteria used for these nominations are that: 1) they should be known by worldly conventions. Thus, what to the speaker is a table should be accepted as a table by the bearer; 2) such conventions should not be contradicted by valid reasoning and cognition; and 3) should not be contradicted by an analysis of its ultimate nature. In the

Buddhist view of ultimate reality, neither any phenomenon nor any self has an inherent existence. They do not exist permanently from their own side. They are 'self-less'.

If we subject a tree to an ultimate analysis of its nature, we find that when we strip it down to its minutest particle, there is no such particle or thing either inside or outside that we can say is the tree. We can define it in terms of its qualities and appearances and say that it is large or small, fragrant or odourless, that a tree has bark, roots, branches and leaves.

We can thus see that a tree can only be defined dependently on other things. From its own side, it has no inherent existence. We can do a similar analysis of the 'I' and 'me' and will find that a search into their ultimate reality reveals that they can only be defined through dependent links; there is no solid and permanent thing that is an 'I' or a 'me'.

In Buddhism, grasping at permanence and believing in the inherent existence of either phenomenon or self is the root delusion. All suffering stems from this delusion. Because the 'I' is deluded of this nature of ultimate reality, it grasps for permanence — of happiness, fame, wealth, beauty, of friends and enemies.

This ignorance creates the first root poison of craving and desire for self-cherishing and self-gratifying values like wealth, fame, beauty, physical pleasures of food, drink and sex. When we are thwarted from achieving these, we create the second root poison of anger and hatred.

Buddha explained that this confusion — our imagining that everything exists in the manner in which our minds give rise to an appearance of it — is the root cause of our troubles. When fortune changes to misfortune, love to hatred, friendship to enmity, our minds give rise to anger, tension, frustration and despair. It does not appear to us that these negative afflictions are not merely the experience of a situation but rather that they are a true and inherent part of the situation itself.

Experience is merely whatever happens to us, whatever occurs. The confused mind views experience that arises of a cognitive contact as permanent, with an inherent existence from its own side. It confuses the experiences and appearances that arise out of beauty, wealth, fame, and power to be of a different substance than those arising out of anger, hatred and despair.

The path that leads to unconfused and clear states of mind is the Dharma way. The state where all suffering has ceased through the cultivation of a clear state of mind is Nirvana.

It's Absolute Bliss, Within & Without

By Purushottam Mahajan

OTHING exists apart from the Absolute. Yet, the Absolute, being transcendent, does not suffer from the limitations of the sense-organs, of attributes, of time. It is imperceivable, eternally pure, unqualified and is bliss. By knowing the Absolute everything is known, and fear and delusion remain no more.

The ultimate resting place exists in the Absolute. It is the knowledge of the Absolute that brings about the fulfilment of the nature of man, and the desire for the experience of Being is characterised by peace.

The world we live in and the world we experience is deeply rooted in what we may call the dialectic or duality. It manifests its nature in terms of rise and fall, birth and death, cause and effect, one and many, here and there, knower and the known, I and you. It is the collectivity of countless dualities that make up the Being in constant flux.

There is nothing in this world that can be said to be permanent. Being subject to its inherent nature, the world is transient and infirm. Blessed are they with the gift of knowledge who realise the unity of Being in the midst of the world of dualities. The knower of the Absolute is one who realises and experiences the same Reality in everything, who finds the presence of Being in life and death, in I and you, in here and there, in a drop of water and in the waters of an ocean, in a small pebble and a mountain, in one and many.

He alone has merged himself in the samata-gnosis of the Absolute who experiences the absence of difference. Gurudeva Mangatramji has explained the basic characteristics of the one who is firmly established in the samata-knowledge of the Absolute. According to him, "The characteristics of the one who realised the evenness or equilibrium of Being are that he is no more tormented either by pleasures or by sorrows, the one in whom the desire for the fruit of action is totally absent, and remain always and constantly established in the presence of own-being.

"He is a person who has achieved the state of total dispassion, for his intellect always remains free from the influence of sense-organs, and experiences both inwardly and outwardly the presence of the self alone. Dualities no more affect him and he remains firmly established in the sameness of the self."

For the ignorant, the multitude of things is real, whereas the knower of the Absolute sees and experiences the presence of unity in the apparent difference. The ordinary person of common sense, being subject to space and time, remains bound to innumerable sense-experiences. He is unable to find the presence of unity in diversity; he is unable to discover the presence of Being in that which is outside of him.

For ordinary men and women, the apparent world of objects is real, and their intellects remain confined to the surface of objective reality. Even the man of natural state can gain some intimations of the Absolute if he succeeds in stabilising his unstable intellect. Only a mind that has gained a certain amount of stability can comprehend that the objects of experience, although the cause of much ill, are not bereft or devoid of Divine presence.

An object becomes the source of ill at that moment when the intellect not only objectifies the object, but also objectifies the Divine presence due to which the object exists. Each object, in fact, does not exist in-itself. As such the objects of perception are non-real. It follows, then, that the intellect that objectifies the non-real objects too is non-real or apparent.

On the disappearance of the object, the intellect too is deprived of the presence of the object. The Divine presence that is immanent in the object of the intellect perishes not with the passing away of the object.

Without the presence of Being, even the existence of the non-real object is not possible. Even though the objects are unreal, their substratum, that is, Brahmn, continues to be. That which is real remains, and the unreal alone is negated. The delight that is derived from the unity of Being remains constant and continuous through the three periods of time.

It is the unchanging Real that is the basis and substratum of the objectivity of objects. The presence of Being exists in equal measure in the expression of each mood. The presence of the Reality exists in same measure in a particle as it exists in a mountain.

The Self is the heart of each object and its presence is even and same in every object. The Self is verily different from the body; the body gets born, decays and dies; the self abides.

Changing Nature of Universe

By Kailash Vajpeyi

HE Zen master, Hakuin, was praised by his neighbours as one living a pure life. A beautiful Japanese girl whose parents owned a food store lived near him. Suddenly, without any warning, her parents discovered she was with child. This made her parents angry. She would not confess who the man was, but after much harassment, at last named Hakuin. In great anger the parents went to the master. "Is that so?" was all he would say.

After the child was born, it was brought to Hakuin. By this time, he had lost his reputation, which did not trouble him, but he took very good care of the child. He obtained milk from his neighbours and everything else the little one needed. A year later the girl-mother could stand it no longer. She told her parents the truth — that the real father of the child was a young man who worked in the fishmarket.

The mother and father of the girl at once went to Hakuin to ask his forgiveness, and to get the child back. Hakuin was willing. In yielding the child, all he said was: "Is that so?"

This story reflects the true Buddha nature. Buddha reached this state of mind after having understood the deeper meaning of suffering, its cause and the doctrine of impermanence.

Conscience has one logic, and fate, another — and these two do not coincide. The uncertainty principle continues to haunt us. Fate does not practise the craft of transgradation. Her wheel is sometimes so fast that we can scarcely distinguish the interval between one revolution and another. Here lies the cause of suffering and working towards its cessation needs a superior vision. This vision is to recognise that the world is not a homogeneous blob, but an integrated network of phenomena linked together in an infinite variety of ways.

Buddha calls it Pratityasamutpad which means 'dependent origination'. A prior function in its own turn serves a causal condition for the emergence of the other function or functions.

Therefore, Buddha repeatedly tells us not to relate to life in fragments but take a holistic approach. Wisdom lies in shedding the false sense of 'I-ness' because it gives rise to the feeling of separateness.

Buddha's idea of total cohesion coincides with J S Bell's mathematical proof, which is known as Bell's theorem — that at a deep and fundamental level the separate parts of the universe are connected in an intimate and immediate way. For years the Buddha starved till he was reduced to a skeleton. But he rejected the notion that self-mortification helps in finding the truth.

When he saw the light, he said: "Come! Practise the method of gaining emancipation that I have discovered. When you have fully accomplished it, you will see the truth face to face, as I see it now."

Most of us take the dictum, 'all things are impermanent', to mean that all existence must eventually die and fade away. The negative aspect of this dictum figures prominently in a number of philosophical systems of our country. But it also has a positive side. If the decline and death of human beings is an example of impermanence, so is birth and growth.

The doctrine of impermanence is a natural, ever-changing phenomenon. Alexis Carrel, who wrote Man the Unknown, goes a step further. According to him, man is constituted by a series of forms following and blending into each other. He is egg, embryo, infant, adolescent, adult, mature and old man. These morphological aspects are the expression of chemical, organic and psychological events. Most of these variations cannot be measured accurately. Therefore, man is a multidimensional creature, who is ever changing. Change is also a fundamental characteristic of the universe. Sakyamuni discovered this principle 2,600 years ago.

Vision-inspired AXN Can Work Wonders

By Swami Tejomayananda

HE quality of our actions and reactions depends upon our vision of life. A narrow vision is divisive. A broad vision is expansive. But, the supreme vision is all inclusive — and the higher the vision, the greater the mission.

Life is a series of perceptions and responses. We are constantly responding to people, situations and events. How we respond depends upon individual perceptions. Different people see the same object, but how each one views it, makes all the difference.

Perception is, therefore, a vision of life and response, an action or reaction, which depends on that vision. Whatever we see or experience with our gross sense organs is alone considered real. The world of names and forms deludes the mind. Everyone finds the world with its infinite variety and exquisite beauty very enchanting.

To understand this world deeply is a difficult task. We see and relate to only superficial objects while the one Truth which pervades the multiple, diverse world remains unseen.

A pure mind and a subtle intellect are required to see this Truth. This is the sattvic vision the Bhagavad Gita talks about. A vision which helps one see unity in the midst of diversity and protects one in the face of temptation, frustration and fear.

The Upanishads exhort us to develop this indivisible, immutable, immaculate vision.

Most people either have a rajasic vision or extroverted outlook, or a tamasic vision or dull approach. A person with a rajasic vision forms mental divisions, such as 'I-my', 'you-yours' or 'good-bad'. He performs actions with either attachment or aversion. He is happy as long as everything is in accordance with his likes and dislikes.

The moment there is a difference, he becomes agitated, angry and troublesome. He inflicts sorrow on a number of people in a very short time because of a lack of vision and absence of noble inspirations.

A man with a tamasic vision is even worse. He is indolent and deeply, fanatically and narrowly attached to a particular object, ideology or cause, with the result that his life is full of conflicts. He looks for happiness through addictions, greed and conflict. To be able to lead a complete and satisfactory life, we need to develop a sattvic vision.

Swami Chinmayananda once said, "You are born, therefore you must die — but don't die while living, live after you are dead." When we hear of a person's demise, we generally ask, "How did he die?" We do not ask, "How did he live?" The focus should be on the kind of life he lived. Was he inspired? Did he inspire others?

Broadly speaking, there are two kinds of lives; one is the life of values and the other is the life of valuables. When people give too much importance to valuables, values are left aside and when values are ignored the person himself gets de-valued.

Meaningless activities without any foundation of vision, knowledge or understanding lead to feverish activity. This, in turn, leads to stress. The imbalance arises because people focus on action, paying scant attention to vision. Dynamism requires a combination of great vision and action to produce results, as it happened when Arjuna was faced with a dilemma on the battlefield.

More than an army, he needed the right vision and advice. Krishna spoke to Arjuna from the spiritual standpoint, taking into account the religious, social and worldly standpoints, giving him a holistic vision. "Look at your life as a whole and live a whole life."

Krishna symbolises the spiritual vision and Arjuna, as the man of action, sets about translating this supreme vision into action. Vision without action remains a concept; action without vision leads to fruitless activity.

Beyond Dianetics And Scientology

By L Ron Hubbard

OR long we have sought freedom from the endless cycle of birth and death. We have looked for personal immortality containing full awareness, memory and ability as a spirit independent of the flesh. The reactive mind and its effect upon the spirit and body makes such permanent freedom difficult to attain.

In scientology, this state has been achieved on a stable plane of full awareness and ability. By getting rid of the reactive mind, we not only achieve erasure of the seeming evil in man, who is basically good, we have overcome the barriers which made it so difficult to attain total spiritual independence and serenity.

We call this state 'Operating Thetan' (OT). To operate something is to be able to handle it. 'Thetan' comes from the Greek letter theta, the traditional philosopher's symbol of thought, spirit or life. An Operating Thetan has "knowing and willing cause over life, thought, matter, energy, space and time".

As man is basically good, despite his evil reactions to his reactive mind, a being who is Clear becomes willing to trust himself with such abilities. No one can have more power than he or she can control. In scientology, a Clear can walk his way to Operating Thetan level within months. And when he attains the state, he is no longer subject to sudden and inexplicable collapses.

One is able to attain and retain the desirable condition. Not the least of the qualities of an OT is personal and knowing immortality and freedom from the cycle of birth and death. The concept is rather vast for immediate grasp — chiefly because hope turns to despair which, in turn, transforms into total apathy. By placing your feet on the first rung of the ladder of dianetics, ascend by scientology to Clear and then walk upward to and far beyond the stars.

The reactive portion of the mind works on a stimulus-response basis which is not under a person's volitional control and which exerts force and power over a person's awareness, purposes, thoughts, body and actions. The technique used in dianetics and scientology is called 'auditing'. Auditing uses processes — exact sets of questions asked or directions given by an auditor to help a person find out things about himself and improve his condition.

There are several different auditing processes, and each one improves the individual's ability to confront and handle part of his existence. When the specific objective of any one process is attained, it is ended and another can then be run to address a different part of the person's life. The questions or directions of the process guide the person to inspect a certain part of his existence. What is found will naturally vary from person to person, since everyone's experiences are different.

Regardless, the individual is assisted in locating not only areas of difficulty, but in locating the source of the upset. By doing this, any person is able to free himself of unwanted barriers that inhibit, stop or blunt his natural abilities and increase these abilities so that he becomes brighter and more able.

Towards Achieving Purity of Spirit

By Acharya Mahaprajna

HE followers of Jainism celebrate Paryushan Parva, a spiritual festival that is spread over 30 days, culminating in the Kshamavani Diwas, the day of forgiveness and atonement. In pursuance of the ultimate goal of Jainism, of achieving spiritual good, these 30 days are characterised by the observance of fasts, vows of silence and meditation. The underlying philosophy is to expound on truths like the impermanence of life.

There are two paths in life, the material and the spiritual. As long as we continue to work only through our conscious mind, we can never truly aspire for perfection. There are four steps to attaining spirituality; contemplation of impermanence, of non-sheltering, of separation of self from the material body and contemplation of solitariness.

By achieving these four kinds of contemplation, we come closer to attaining spirituality. Mere repetition of certain words or chanting alone does not make one spiritual. The harsh reality is that with the present mental, physical and emotional conditions, we can never realise either our soul or our existence.

By practising the four-fold spiritual process we can realise ourselves. The first step towards realisation begins with the practice of impermanence of matter. By practising this, gradually, the happiness and sorrow associated with the object will start annihilating. An undesirable object gives sorrow, and a desirable object gives happiness. But in the state of intense awareness of impermanence, there is no sorrow.

When the truth about the acquisition and separation of an object is fully understood, then there is no sorrow. When this consciousness awakens with full realisation, then there is no more fear and suffering of old age or death. A person who lives realistically and in spirituality with full realisation, can transcend these sufferings and enjoy unobstructed and infinite bliss.

What is sambodhi or enlightenment? It is the witnessing or awareness of impermanence. Basically, enlightenment is of three types: enlightenment of knowledge, vision and conduct. Intellect is also of three kinds: intellect of knowledge, vision and conduct. Witnessing is also of three kinds: witnessing of knowledge, reality and conduct.

The first step of spirituality is the witnessing of impermanence. A spiritual person is one "who has witnessed the impermanent". The second element is nonsheltering. The helpless state of sickness and intense pain can awaken the consciousness of nonsheltering in anyone. External materials cannot provide relief and shelter.

Therefore, we should seek shelter within ourselves. There are basically two kinds of persons, external seekers and internal seekers. A spiritual person is an internal seeker. An external seeker is materialistic because he is always inclined to seek externally. He searches for the solution to every problem in the material world. He hankers after objects.

It is natural that wherever you are inclined, you will always move in that direction only. If your tendency is to seek within, you will surely seek the solution to every problem in your spirit. We are deeply attached to our physical body. Our delusion is so profound and deep that we have accepted the body and soul to be the same. As long as this thinking persists, spirituality cannot materialise.

The philosophy of contemplation of separation from the body is that, when knowledge of the separation of the soul from the body awakens, then spirituality starts taking root.

We accept three traits of personality: memory, imagination and thinking. All the three are mechanical and not related to the soul. Feeling is related to the soul. It cannot be mechanical.

The one who realises happiness and sorrow, exists. When the consciousness of the separation from the body awakens, then only does spirituality commence.

The last step of spirituality is to be solitary. Mahavira has attached great importance to meditation in a solitary state.

A person who has learnt the art of experiencing solitude even while in a crowd, has learnt to lead a life free from tension. The practice of spirituality should be pragmatic and rational, like the four contemplations talked about in Jainism. In the context of

Prekshadhyana, we have accepted 16 types of contemplations. Each contemplation is practised for months together and only then are they assimilated in our life. Perception and contemplation should be practised together to attain happiness, to help us refine our thoughts and purify our mind.

Way to Remember Your Loved Ones

By Simi Bajaj

T can happen to anyone. Destiny can strike suddenly, changing your life forever. God has plans for everyone. The wisdom and kindness of God is beyond our minds' reach. We can only try to understand it if we surrender totally to God and have deep faith. The way to deal with crisis and life-threatening situations is to resolve to do our best and let God do the rest...

When there is birth, there will be death too. It is the universal law of nature, yet the human mind does not want to accept this truth. When a loved one dies, our minds become numb. We want to cling on, we refuse to let go... because of our worldly attachments and relationships.

Krishna says in Gita: "For the soul, there is neither birth nor death. Nor, having once been, does he ever cease to be. He is unborn, eternal, ever existing, undying and primeval. He is not slain when the body is slain."

I sense with deep emotion, an age-old truth that crying, a human enters this world — and on leaving, leaves behind so many in tears. The way to remember your loved ones, who have quit the race of life, is to make their loss your strength, so that it transforms into the power that makes you strive.

Death is the unwelcome visitor, and often comes unannounced. For some it is painful; for others, too sudden. There are souls waiting for death, there are souls escaping from death. Each one is bound up in his own cycle of karma, even from previous births. So it is as important to have a dream as it is to nurture it. Life reveals its moments of truth/ Destiny unveils scene by scene/ Winners are those in the race of life/ Who have the faith to follow their dream.../ God has plans for everyone/ Karma reigns powerful and supreme/ Blessed are those who listen to their hearts/ And have the passion to follow their dream.../ Many a time, you will swim against the tide/ Many a time will relationships fail/ But do not

132

stop pursuing your dream/ Strive ahead and etch your writing on the wall.

The death of a loved one can throw you into deep depression, and can wreck you emotionally, physically, mentally. But remember, there is not a single person out there, who has not suffered this pain. Death is universal. Dealing with the loss of a loved one is not easy; you have to, however, face it by holding your wits together. For yesterday is history, tomorrow a mystery, today is the most important of all.

Live every moment to the full... who knows when God might call? When my little son died, I was devastated. I was tempted to give in to emotions of revenge, anger, resentment and burning fury. Could this turmoil in me bring back my son alive? No.

It was difficult, but I chose to follow the path of love, kindness and good karma. Why let the loss of a loved one go in vain? Why should deep despair increase the gnawing pain? It is better to illuminate your heart and soul with memories of your shining star — and you will realise the truth, that heaven is not really that far.

There comes a turning point in everybody's life. My little son's demise has made me treat this painful loss as a stepping stone to spiritual evolvement. Breaking the emotional tie, I have removed all the worldly pictures of the cute toddler, and instead, installed the idol of Balgopal Krishna, God Almighty, in the mandir at my home, who is the object of our devotion and affection.

I prefer to think of my son as the little angel who came to bless and touch our lives forever. In honour of his memory — I shall enrich my life and that of others with faith, good karma and prayer.

When It's Time, Let Go of Life

By T Rajagopalachari

EATH is an enigma. It is impossible to define life without death. Up to its very last link, life is a bio-chemical chain reaction. Once life is launched, like a bullet it must reach its final destination, which is death. Death is less frightening, however, when we concede that life attains maximum fullness only when it is guided by an ideal, by something for which we are willing to die if necessary. Whatever incites us to die also incites us to live with greater intensity. That's why the lives of heroes, mystics and martyrs are more intense than the life of an ordinary mortal. That's also why love and the pleasures of the senses are felt more intensely by people who are facing death in a war or revolution.

When I was young, a World War II veteran who was lucky to escape many bomb attacks in Burma (now Myanmar) told me that for those of them who were living in the expectation of dying at any moment, everything — a day of sunshine, the warm clasp of a friendly hand, a pretty face, a colourful bird, a rose — acquired a sublime and unexpected value.

A noble example of a serene attitude towards death is to be found in the last letters that Dr Wilson, physician, naturalist, artist and Antarctic explorer, wrote to his wife from the icy wastes of the South Pole. The men in Scott's ill-fated expedition — of which Dr Wilson was a member — were starving, had no fuel with which to keep warm.

Dr Wilson's letters were found near his ice-sheathed body. "Don't be unhappy", he wrote. "We are playing a good part in the great scheme arranged by God himself... We will all meet after death, and death has no terrors..."

The roots of fear of death are fear of pain and of the feeling of anguish that is implicit in dying, and the sadness of leaving loved ones and joys that bind us to the world.

Third, and perhaps most important, is fear of the unknown.

Death, with exceptions, is not accompanied by physical pain. Rather, it is suffused with serenity, even a certain well-being and spiritual exaltation, caused by the anaesthetic action of carbon dioxide on the central nervous system.

Science reveals that the sensation of dying is like that of falling asleep. And if a person accepts his death as an act of service to an ideal, or as the end of his life's work, it could be a blessing. It could be accepted more willingly if we knew that we had fulfilled our duty in life.

Fear of the unknown is similar to the childhood fear of darkness. Does our protoplasm simply dissolve into its primordial elements and return to the universe, or does the complex system of images that we call consciousness survive? Carl Jung said, "The decisive question is: Are we related to something infinite or not? Only if we know that the thing which truly matters is the infinite can we avoid fixing our interest upon futilities and upon all kinds of goals which are not of real importance."

Just as we cultivate the will to live, we should cultivate the will to shed our mortal coils properly. We desire death only in moments of utter desperation. Were we to deem it a physiological necessity like hunger or thirst, we would aspire to die, as Nietzsche said, "Like a torch which dies exhausted and glutted with relief."

Even as a coin attains its full value when it is spent, so life attains its supreme value when one knows how to forfeit it with grace when the time comes.

Finality of Death is a Myth

By Ruby Lilaowala

N literature, art and cinema, death has been almost always depicted as a terrible thing, the final end, although in reality it is merely a release from the burden of the physical body. Every religious tradition recognises that to reach the final truth, one must pass through death. This is the meaning behind Aanea's descent to the underworld in Virgil, of Dante's descent into hell in the Divine Comedy and the Christian baptism: "You were baptised into the death of Christ."

In the Katha Upanishad, Nachiketa asks Yama, "What lies beyond death?" The Upanishad states: "The wise man, who, by meditation on the self recognises the ancient, who is difficult to be seen, who has entered into the dark, who is seated in a cave, who dwells in the abyss, just as God, who has left both joy and sorrow, friends and foes behind, has already known what lies beyond death."

Death is merely the loss of the physical body which is a piece of cloth to cover the soul. After death, the mental and emotional states are as active as ever. In the Chandogya Upanishad, there's a description of the four stages of consciousness: Jagrat or wakefulness, Swapna or dream-state, Turya or meditative-state and Sushupti or the highest state of awareness.

A topic with which each and every human being is concerned with and yet remains amazingly ignorant of, is the topic of life and death and their relationship. Plato, in his discourse with Socrates, asked: "Is it simply the release of the soul from the body? Is death nothing more or less than this, the separate condition of the body by itself when it is released from the soul, and the separate condition by itself of the soul when released from the body?"

All major religions of the world affirm that there is a subtle and death-surviving element, vital and psychical in the physical body of flesh and blood, whether it is the permanent entity of self, such as the Brahmanic atma of the Hindus, the Islamic ruh, the Christian-Judaic soul, or a complex of activities with life as their function according to the Buddhist concept. Thus, to none of these faiths is death an absolute ending. It is merely the separation of the psyche from the gross-body.

The ancient Egyptian Book of the Dead refers to death as "the snapping of the silver-cord". Death remains a tragedy, a problem, a heart-rending experience and a source of great suffering though it has existed since eternity. Why? As long as there is identification with and dependence on the external form, the gross physical body, as the only reality, death is tragic. However, if consciousness can be focused beyond the external form and labels (i.e. the labels of father, mother, son, daughter, etc) then death loses its terror.

In every religion we find guidelines on how to move from life to death. Tibetans have the Bardo Thodol or the Book of the Dead, which gives instructions on how to condition the next birth through mental yoga — of course, within the limitations of karma. In Zoroastrian religious literature, it is stated that "every tear shed for the departed soul becomes a raging astral-river which retards the spiritual progress of that soul".

Not surprisingly, in Celtic death ceremonies, there is dancing and feasting signifying joy at the departed soul's liberation. Similarly, neo-pagan death rituals are a form of celebration, accompanied by music and presents of rice and flowers for the departed.

In James Barrie's Peter Pan, Peter says, "To die will be an awfully big adventure." So also in J R Tolkein's Lord of The Rings: The protagonist Frodo boards death's ship to heaven when he "heard the sound of singing by his friends on earth".

Just as we have a physical body, we have a mental body, an emotional body, an energy body and a subtle body (sukshma-sharir). All these bodies cover the soul or atma like sheaths (or layers of an onion). But once you realise that you are the soul (atma-swaroop) and not any of the other bodies, then you have gone beyond time and space and, consequently, beyond birth and death.

The subtle body is the electro-magnetic body (aura) that permeates the physical body and extends beyond it in space. During the process of death, the subtle body gradually starts to withdraw from the physical body, and when this process is completed, the soul (atma) withdraws from the subtle body.

It was this moment which was referred to as "the snapping of the silver cord" by initiates of the ancient mysteries in Egypt.

Existential Dilemma:
What is Life?

By Kailash Vajpeyi

XISTENTIALISM begins as a voice raised in protest against the absurdity of pure thought, according to the critics of western philosophy. It has its roots in the works of Soren Kierkegaard, a 19th century Danish theologian-philosopher and author of Either/Or and Concluding Unscientific Postscript.

He said that truth lies in subjectivity. So an objective study of truth is impossible. He also considered existence as a system which has its finality. Man at his best is existent and persistently striving to become something; man is in the process of 'becoming'. Truth is never realised as long as the experiencer is alive. "Life can only be explained after it has been lived, just as Christ only began to interpret the scriptures and how they applied to him — after his resurrection." Moreover, the person who is making some such effort should not be absent-minded or a madman.

Truth is a very serious subjective experience for each individual. Is life utterly meaningless? Kierkegaard would often ask in despair. His basic dilemma was his own existence. "How did I come into the world? Why was I not consulted? Why was I not acquainted with its manner and customs, but was thrust into the ranks as though I had been bought from a kidnapper, a dealer in souls? And if I am compelled to take part in this play where is the director? I would like to see him," he wrote. Kierkegaard also wanted to give a new meaning to Christianity. His argument deals with the object of Christian faith and the manner of approaching it.

"That a man born and living history says he is God and dies in humiliation — and plunges into a dilemma, and that there are those who would build their lives on his word... Nothing has happened since to lighten by one scruple the strain of belief. The historical success of Christianity is worthless evidence," he said. Basically, a man of religious temperament, the Danish thinker felt that the purpose of seeking the truth is to exist in it — not to think about it. "In the strict sense, being a Christian means to die to the world and then be sacrificed."

With Kierkegaard it is said his thought swung back to the days of Socrates who believed that the body is the enemy of your thought. So the philosopher's main aim should be death. Inspired by the theses of truth and subjectivity propounded by Kierkegaard, Karl Jaspers, a psycho-pathologist, explored the theme of existence while analysing the core of human consciousness. He laid emphasis on authentic living which, he said, is revealed in such crucial situations as the awareness of death.

Philosophy must return to the question of being, wrote Martin Heidegger, the author of Being and Time. For being would throw light on human existence. Like T S Eliot who asked: " Where is the time we have lost in living?"

Heidegger also talks of being that degrades itself in mediocrity. Existentialist Jean Paul Sartre wrote: "God is a useless and costly hypothesis; so we will do without it." It is true that 'man is a useless passion' and suffers from the 'anguish of Abraham'. Nevertheless, if we are to have a cohesive society and a law-abiding world, it is essential that certain values should be taken seriously, they must have an a priori existence ascribed to them.

Put Life and Death
In Perspective

By Asit M Kaushik

EARS ago when I first saw Hrishikesh Mukherjee's timeless classic Anand, I was deeply affected by this line spoken by the protagonist: "Babumoshai, zindagi badi honi chahiye, lambi nahin!" The words have lived with me ever since.

They echo Oscar Wilde's words: " It doesn't matter how long, but how you live!"

The concept of death as an inevitability is so ancient that it has been reduced to a cliche. We all know we are going to die, but for some reason, are unwilling to accept this fact.

Deep inside our psyche is rooted the idea that while death may come to others, we will somehow continue to live forever. And on account of this belief alone, we attach undue importance to material possessions by becoming selfish, vain and arrogant.

Poet Kabir epitomised the futility of arrogance thus: "Don't be so proud and vain/ for the clutches of time are dark/ Nobody knows where it might strike, whether at home or outside!" Reports say that many of the 9/11 survivors are relentlessly preaching the worthlessness of material acquisitions and the importance of love and compassion for all.

We become conscious of death only when it occurs in our vicinity and claims those who are dear to us. At all other times we remain in a state of blissful ignorance. In Indian folklore, there's this story of a woman who took her debauched son to meet Buddha. On seeing the youth, Buddha told him that he had just one more day to live. The youngster was shocked, but knew there was little that he could do about Buddha's prediction.

Having realised that time was so short, he clung to his mother's sari, and broke down. He wanted to meet all his family members, friends and neighbours before the end came.

With six hours left for his death, he found himself lying on a cot, distraught and disillusioned.

When just three hours were left, Buddha paid him a visit. The youth did not wish to speak to Buddha, but the latter smiled at him and inquired if in the last 24 hours, he had lied or cheated. The youth replied in the negative. Buddha then asked him if he had stolen from or hurt anybody. The youth got irritated and replied that how could he possibly think of doing such things when all he was thinking of was death.

Buddha gently patted his head and said: "Son, I don't know who has to die and who has to live, but understanding the ultimate truth can be very enlightening. While you became aware of death only in the last 24 hours, I have been aware of it for the last 24 years."

Fear of death stems from our fear of seeing it all end, losing our possessions and being catapulted into endless darkness. Most people find it difficult to come to terms with their mortality; they prefer to believe that there is life even after death. But those who are in constant touch with their inner spirit seldom fear the inevitable. They believe in neither heaven nor hell; they also don't believe in the theory of incarnation.

Our stipulated lifespan is a mere 'blip' in this ostensibly vast eternity spanning billions of years. We must, therefore, learn to value each day of our life and savour it, moment by moment. All those who believe in hoarding their energy and resources for the future could take a cue from the insatiable musician who eventually rued: "I spent so much time in stringing my instruments that there was no time left for me to perform..."

Looking Beyond Life and Death

By Chitranjan Sawant

ONG years ago in the Kashmir valley, the Purohit of the Arya Samaj was blessed with a daughter. When she was three or four years old, she told her parents that she belonged to a village in the valley and was the daughter of a senior officer of the Jammu and Kashmir government. She insisted on being taken to the village of her previous birth. Her parents obliged. On reaching the village, she identified her friends, relatives as well as property.

However, relatives from her previous life as well as her present-day parents chose to discourage her from visiting the old sites. Over a period of time, memories of the previous life were obliterated.

There is no scientific explanation to an event of this nature, such cases do happen but they are few and far between. However, this does give an indication that our present life is not our first life and, in any case, not the last one.

Krishna, while boosting the morale of Arjuna just before the start of Mahabharat, told him that this was neither his first life nor his last one. Even if a warrior is slain in battle, it is only the body that perishes and not the soul. The soul finds another body sooner rather than later. Krishna said that he remembered his previous lives but a man in this mundane world does not.

Otherwise, confusion would be worst confounded. Many a senior citizen here and elsewhere, thinks of the other world, having played his innings in this world. Having lived beyond the Biblical 'three scores and ten', it would be in the fitness of things were the elderly to fathom the depth of our scriptures and find what these have to say about life beyond death. Let there be no anxiety about the fate that awaits senior citizens when they go into eternal sleep.

The question of life beyond death has been addressed well in the Vedic thought.

Jeevem Sharadah Shatam is a man's prayer to his maker. Men and women beseech God for a Vedic life span of 100 years wherein they are not bereft of health and happiness. Men and women are encouraged in the Vedic way of life to be active in their respective spheres till the last breath so that they court death cheerfully when it arrives.

Life is more than just passing time. Vedic prayers exhort human beings to even go beyond celebrating their centenary in this world. One who lives a full life will never be afraid of death, may it come in any form, under any circumstances.

"If winter comes, can spring be far behind," says Keats at the height of his optimism. There is always hope for a better future, maybe in this world or maybe in the next world. Bad days are certainly to be followed by good days, like day follows night. This is why a pragmatist sounds a note of caution for the future and says: Ye all, who have lived life, now should be prepared to court death.

All major religions of the world agree on the inevitability of this life coming to an end in this world. One who is born is bound to die. Vedic philosophy says that the real self of a man is not his body but the soul. The phenomena of birth and death pertain to the body only and not to the soul. The soul is immortal. Na Hanyate Hanyamane Sharire, that is, on being slain it is only the body that perishes and the soul survives, says Lord Krishna who based his pronouncements on the knowledge of the Vedas.

The immortality of the soul as well as the transmigration of the soul is underlined time and again. There is equal emphasis on the present life as on life beyond death: Let all men and women assure and reassure themselves: I am not the body, I am the soul. The soul is neither born nor does it die. Pray, in that case, what is birth and what is death?

Well, when a soul enters a body it is called birth. And when the same soul departs from the body, it is called death. This process goes on and on. The cycle of birth and death or transmigration of soul comes to an end only when the soul attains moksha or liberation from this cycle. This may be termed as salvation of the soul.

William Wordsworth, the poet, was bold enough to believe in a life beyond death. He succeeded in keeping pessimism at bay by drawing inspiration from the belief that the soul had its beginning elsewhere and lived endlessly. Indeed, it is a cheering thought for the senior citizens that the sunset that awaits them will soon be followed by a sunrise.

Break Free from Fear of Death

By Pramod Pathak

EATH perhaps is the only certainty in this world. Yet, the fear of death stalks most people. Literature — western and Indian — regards the fear of death as an intriguing and ubiquitous part of human life. We know we are mortals, yet we are afraid of the inevitable. We know we will die one day; yet we continue to behave as though we believe we are going to live forever.

In Shakespeare's Julius Caesar, Caesar is surprised to find that people are frightened of death, which is after all an end that comes when it will. A similar spirit pervades the renowned dialogue between the Yaksha and Yudhishthira in the Mahabharata.

When the Yaksha asked him what is the greatest surprise, Yudhishthira replied that so many people die everyday. Yet, human beings want to somehow avoid death. That, he said, was truly surprising. However, for people of knowledge, for the wise, death is the door to liberation, the passage to moksha. Few understand the concept of moksha — it is the conscious concern of those who strive for freedom from bondage. Their goal is not more security or pleasure; it is to achieve freedom from all desire.

Moksha is the end of all desire leading to freedom from the cycle of birth and death.

Of the four purusharthas, moksha is the noblest. The other three are: dharma, artha and kama. These are sought by ordinary people. Moksha, however, is the goal of the wise.

For many, liberation becomes the goal only when the limitations of the other three purusharthas are realised. But by then it is too late.

We spend all our lives in the pursuit of pleasure, wealth and fame. Finally, we realise that nothing gives us fulfilment. The joy is momentary, proving that our efforts were futile, unsatisfactory and incomplete. True joy lies in completeness and limitlessness, the path to liberation. Moksha ensures liberation from all limitations that bind human beings.

Man's constant struggle to achieve happiness through acquiring security and pleasure is bound to fail, for, these efforts are generally misdirected. This is because the nature of the fundamental problem is not understood fully. The road to freedom from limitations is to be found only in the correct knowledge of one's true nature as that which is absolute.

Salvation lies in merging with this absolute and the doorway for this is death. But there are several hurdles: ignorance and incomplete knowledge of the concept of death as the beginning of the final journey. To come out of this ignorance, spiritual inspiration is required.

Without such motivation, self-realisation needed for attainment of moksha cannot be achieved. But how to prepare for moksha?

The first step is to develop self-control. This will lead to freedom from attachment to objects. A real seeker of moksha has to be a sanyasi. However, it is not necessary to renounce the world to be a sanyasi. All one has to do is switch off mental preoccupations with objects of the world. Living amidst worldly objects without feeling attached to them is true vairagya.

The second step is the abandonment of aham, the thought of 'I'. Tat Twam Asi — That Thou Art — is something that's central to Indian philosophy. One must come to live in one's own divine nature. Indifference to objects of the senses, to feelings of pain and pleasure and also absence of egoism help make the mind steady.

The Bhagavad Gita calls this state sthitapragya. This is the crucial state for attaining moksha. The following verse illustrates this concept well: "O build your ship of death.../ O build it now, for you will need it,/ for the voyage of oblivion awaits you."

Fear Not Death, It's Integral to Life

By Parmarthi Raina

EATH is a great equaliser. It reduces everyone — the powerful and the weak, the rich and the poor, the healthy and the sick, the young and the old — equally to a mere inert corpse, a mass of decaying, putrefying flesh and bones. The one thing certain in this material universe is death.

Death overcomes everyone and everything. It gives no warning and can strike down anyone at anytime. Vedic scriptures liken life to a drop of rainwater on a lotus leaf. Poet Tennyson wrote: "Death is the end of life; ah! why should life all labour be?" And existentialist Jean Paul Satre maintained that death made life meaningless. Yet, in search of happiness, man toils and struggles all his life accumulating wealth and material assets in order to fulfil his desires and gratify his senses, under the illusion that with these he can find happiness.

And yet, paradoxically, man is mortally afraid to leave this world. He is afraid to give up his material possessions, his loved ones and his unfulfilled ambitions; afraid of the unknown and afraid of the retributions that possibly await him for his indiscretions and wrongdoings. He, therefore, wants to cling on to his ephemeral body no matter what.

Even when terminally ill he wants to prolong life rather than accept death. Yudhistra, the eldest of the Pandava brothers, when asked as to what was the most amazing thing in this world, replied, "That man sees people dying all around him every day, every moment, yet he thinks that he is not going to die!" Man's intellect may accept that life is transient but the ego does not, and man lives his life thinking it permanent.

Ancient societies of Vedic India, Pharaonic Egypt, South America and Greece, and even some societies of the pre-industrial era, devoted considerable time contemplating on death and the concept of life after death. But modern life has created an ethos

146

where material achievement, economic prosperity and sense gratification are man's main pursuits and so busy and preoccupied is he with living that he seldom thinks about, or contemplates on, the inescapable reality of death.

There is an almost hysterical obsession for haste to do whatever it takes to enjoy life to the full and satiate all sensual desires in the short lifespan available to us, often overlooking ethical and moral codes of behaviour and entirely oblivious to karmic consequences.

In Vedanta, death is the beginning of a new life, a life designed and structured by one's own karmas. It is, therefore, as important to understand death as life itself. Death is an integral part of life, and knowledge of what lies beyond death vital to attain spiritual enlightenment.

Nachiketa, in the Katha Upanishad, obtained it from Yamaraja, the King of Death. The Vedas assert that, unlike the body, the true self, the soul (atma), is eternal and not subject to death. Krishna says in the Bhagawad Gita, "That which pervades the entire body you should know to be indestructible. No one is able to destroy that imperishable soul. He can never be cut to pieces by any weapon, nor burned by fire, nor moistened by water, nor withered by the wind. He is unbreakable, insoluble, everlasting, present everywhere, unchangeable, immovable and eternally the same. With death, the soul merely discards the old body and acquires a new one." The Vedas give great importance to one's thoughts at the moment of death. Krishna says, "Whatever state of being one remembers when he quits his body, O son of Kunti, that state he will attain without fail." Most people would invariably think of their possessions, their relationships and their unfulfilled ambitions. They are then born again in circumstances that would give them opportunities to achieve their desires.

Krishna also says, "Whoever, at the end of his life, quits his body, remembering Me alone, at once attains to My nature, of this there is no doubt." To think of the Lord as one exhales his last breath, however, is possible only if one has consciously remembered Him regularly throughout one's life. One should, therefore, reflect on the inevitability of death and life's impermanent and inane nature and resolutely fix his mind on the Lord. It is only by His grace that man can escape from the vice-like grip of samsara.

The World's a Stage: We're Mere Players

By K S Ram

LL the world's a stage, and all the men and women merely players: They have their exits and their entrances...", wrote William Shakespeare. Shakespeare saw the world as a large theatre. If all the world is indeed a stage, and life is a play, and all of us are mere actors, this view leads to some interesting corollaries.

Who is the author and the director of this play? Obviously, God. The Indian view that creation is God's leela — play — supports this view. What do birth and death signify? Birth corresponds to "Enter" and death to "Exit" in a play. Feeble-minded people in the world often lose courage in life and commit suicide. This extreme step, in terms of theatre, is like an actor losing his head and abruptly walking off the stage in a huff even before his part in the play has ended. Murder, similarly, is like someone pushing a fellow-actor off the stage to stop him from further participation in the drama.

Both are tantamount to disrupting the play, and so amounts to corrupting the script of God. Little wonder, therefore, that all religions unequivocally denounce both murder and suicide as vile sins. A play has all kinds of characters: king, nobleman, peasant, tradesman and more. All are equally dear to the author. All combine to contribute to the total effect of the drama. Nobody is superior, nor is anybody inferior merely by virtue of her calling in life.

Excellence depends on how well you discharge your duty, rather than on how 'exalted' a duty you have been called to discharge. This brings to mind the significance of swa-dharma — one's native calling — in life.

Dwelling on this point, Krishna declares: "One's own dharma, though imperfect, is better than the dharma of another well discharged... Full of fear is the dharma of another."

Illustrating the truth of this verse, Ramakrishna Paramahamsa observes, "A professional farmer does not lose courage and he continues to cultivate even if there be a terrible drought for 12 long years. But a weaver who takes to tilling for a change of occupation gets disheartened if rain fails for one season."

An actor in a play conforms to the script, which represents the will of the author-playwright, just as a person in life should surrender to the will of God. Such surrender is the supreme act of religion, according to Islam.

Likewise, "Thy will be done, O Lord!" is the essence of the Christian's daily prayer. We should accept the will of God, whatever it be, with an humble 'Amen'. Actors on the stage may fight, kill or love, but nothing disturbs their deeper mental state. They never forget that it is a play after all, and that they are simply and faithfully enacting the author's script. They always remain detached. This is equilibrium born of knowledge. How would a person be, if she successfully adopts this condition of equilibrium in actual life?

Krishna says: "He who is the same to foe and friend and also in honour and dishonour, who is the same in cold and heat, in pleasure and pain, who is free from attachment, to whom censure and praise are equal, who is silent — uncomplaining — content with anything, homeless, steady-minded, full of devotion — that man is dear to me."

The essence of the teaching of the Gita is to transform karma into karma yoga: to be active in body but detached in mind. This, in fact, is how any good actor conducts herself on stage.

Death At My Doorstep

By Khushwant Singh

E do not talk of death lightly — it is regarded as tasteless, ill-mannered and depressing. But death is an essential fact of life which makes no exceptions: It comes to kings as well as beggars, to the rich and the poor, to saints as well as sinners, the aged and the young. You simply cannot turn a blind eye to it and fool yourself into believing that death comes to other people but will spare you. It will not. It is best to prepare yourself for it and when it comes, welcome it with a smile on your lips.

Alfred Tennyson wrote: "Sunset and evening star/ And one clear call for me!/ May there be no moaning of the bar/ When I put out to sea.../ ...Twilight and evening bell,/ After that the dark!/ And may there be no sadness of farewell/ When I embark."

I am now over 90 years old and am aware that the hour of my tryst with destiny is drawing near. I have given a lot of thought to it. Being a rationalist, I do not accept irrational, unproven theories of life-death-rebirth in different forms as an unending process till our beings mingle with God and we attain nirvana. I do not accept the belief that while the body perishes, the soul survives. I do not know what the soul looks like; neither I, nor anyone has seen it. Nor do I accept the Hebrew, Christian and Islamic belief in the Day of Judgement — heaven and hell. I go along with poet Mirza Asadullah Khan Ghalib: "We know what the reality of paradise is;/ but it is not too bad an idea to beguile the mind."

I accept the finality of death; we do not know what happens to us after we die... I once asked the Dalai Lama, "Your Holiness, I cannot accept your belief in reincarnation. There is no scientific evidence to support it." The Dalai Lama narrated stories of children who remembered things about their previous existence: names of parents and places where they were born... I interrupted him. "Your Holiness, these are infantile fantasies of children brought up in Hindu, Jain, Buddhist or Sikh families where they hear elders talking of previous life and next life. Can you give me an example of a Muslim child recalling his earlier existence?" The Dalai Lama roared with laughter and replied: "You have a point, but if I did not believe in reincarnation, I would be out of business!"

I have never subscribed to the belief that nothing bad should be said about the dead. If people were evil in their lifetimes, death does not convert them into saints. Such falsehoods may be condoned when inscribed on tombstones but not in obituaries which should be without bias, and truthful. I have written lots of obituaries about people I admired and loved; I have also written about people I detested and loathed. I did my best to be as even-handed as I could about all of them...

Very few people have dates with death apart from those who take their own lives or are convicted by courts to hang. The old and the ailing may sense the day drawing near but never know exactly what day or time it will be... We must always bear in mind that death is inevitable. Memento mori — remember you must die. Without brooding over it, be prepared for it. Ghalib put it beautifully: "Age travels at a galloping pace/ Who knows where it will stop?/ We do not have the reins in our hands/ We do not have our feet in the stirrups."